Cleopatra

ANCIENTS IN ACTION

Catullus
Amanda Hurley

Cleopatra
Susan Walker and Sally-Ann Ashton

Horace
Philip Hills

Lucretius
John Godwin

Ovid: love songs
Genevieve Liveley

Ovid: myth and metamorphosis
Sarah Annes Brown

Spartacus
Theresa Urbainczyk

Tacitus
Rhiannon Ash

ANCIENTS IN ACTION

CLEOPATRA

Susan Walker and Sally-Ann Ashton

BRISTOL CLASSICAL PRESS

First published in 2006 by
Gerald Duckworth & Co. Ltd.
90-93 Cowcross Street, London EC1M 6BF
Tel: 020 7490 7300
Fax: 020 7490 0080
inquiries@duckworth-publishers.co.uk
www.ducknet.co.uk

A catalogue record for this book is available
from the British Library

ISBN 1 85399 673 4
EAN 9781853996733

Typeset by e-type, Liverpool
Printed and bound in Great Britain by
CPI Bath

Contents

Preface and Acknowledgements

Queen Cleopatra VII of Egypt committed suicide rather than submit to her Roman enemy Octavian exactly 2035 years ago.

Our starting point for this short introduction to the last queen of Egypt is her continued significance to a modern public, who mostly know Cleopatra through the medium of film. We note the origins of the Hollywood Cleopatra in the orientalist imagination of nineteenth-century writers and artists, and show how these ideas of Cleopatra draw upon a hostile tradition developed in the last years of the queen's life by her Roman enemies. In contrast, we explore the very positive image Cleopatra has enjoyed since antiquity in Egypt. We also note the nineteenth-century American roots of the recently promoted idea of Cleopatra as black African.

We recount the major events of Cleopatra's extraordinary life, setting her behaviour in the historic context of Ptolemaic Egypt and its relations with Rome, and focusing upon the major players in the fall of the independent kingdom of Egypt to Rome.

Reviewing the range of images of Cleopatra created for – and by – various peoples within the Greek and Roman world, we end by considering at some length the lesser-known repertoire of surviving images of Cleopatra from Egypt itself.

These last are set within the context of Cleopatra's known building programmes.

We are very grateful to Helen Strudwick (Cambridge), Ellen Rice (Oxford) and John Wilkes (Norfolk and Oxford) for reading and commenting on drafts of the manuscript. Our editor Deborah Blake has been the soul of patience as we have struggled to finish the book while adapting to our new posts. We remain responsible for any remaining errors and omissions.

Authors' note: special acknowledgement

We have learned much from our colleagues in the British Museum, and in our present posts at the Ashmolean and Fitzwilliam Museums in the universities of Oxford and Cambridge. The book is a distillation of research undertaken at the British Museum for the major international exhibition *Cleopatra of Egypt: from History to Myth,* held at the Palazzo Ruspoli in Rome in 2000/2001, the British Museum in London in 2001, and the Field Museum in Chicago from 2001-2. Those colleagues who contributed to the international conference held while the exhibition was in London will see some of their published work recast here for a more general readership. We acknowledge their work in the detailed list of articles for further reading cited at the rear of this volume.

Susan Walker
Department of Antiquities, Ashmolean Museum, University of Oxford

Preface and Acknowledgements

Sally-Ann Ashton
Department of Antiquities, Fitzwilliam Museum, University
of Cambridge

April 2006

Illustrations

Figures

From Heroic Suicide to Banknote Icon: Modern Views of Cleopatra

It could be said of the last queen of Egypt that every age gets the Cleopatra it deserves. For many mature adults in western societies today, Elizabeth Taylor, star of Joseph L. Mankiewicz's 1963 film, *is* Cleopatra (Plate 1). Who could forget that triumphal entry scene, that knowing, conspiratorial wink of the violet eye, that pampered flesh luxuriating in the bath of asses' milk and honey? No less memorable was the eruption of Taylor's and her co-star Richard Burton's lives into an affair apparently as passionate and notorious as that enjoyed in antiquity by Cleopatra and Mark Antony.

Burton and Taylor's epic is over forty years old. For many early twenty-first-century audiences, notably but not exclusively in the United States of America, Cleopatra has in the intervening years metamorphosed into an empowering black superwoman, the cunning Egyptian queen appropriately recreated as a CIA agent of legendary skill and wit. The film *Cleopatra Jones* and its sequel *Cleopatra Jones and the Casino of Gold* offer amusing references to Mankiewicz's epic, thereby effectively mocking the dominant view of Cleopatra as white.

Indeed in the ivory towers beyond Hollywood, the black queen has become the stuff of academic controversy, a pawn in the argument advanced by those 'Afrocentrists' who see

Cleopatra as the leading representative of ancient black Africa, and the latter as a far greater force in cultural history than their opponents have allowed. On the other side of the divide, the traditional 'Eurocentrist' historians versed in the cultures of Greece, Mesopotamia and Egypt – the last significantly separated from black Africa – maintain the traditional view of Cleopatra's ethnic identity as a Macedonian Greek. They see any claim for Cleopatra to represent Africa's influence on the development of the ancient world as at best a tendentious reading, at worst a wilful distortion of the surviving evidence.

Far from being the product of recent feminism and the Black Power movement, as is often supposed by those opposed to Afrocentrist interpretations of ancient history, the seeds of Cleopatra's incarnation as a black leader were sown surprisingly long ago. In the America of the 1860s, the time of the Civil War, the last queen of Egypt became an icon for the white liberal writer Nathaniel Hawthorne and the artist William Wetmore Story, who had personally committed themselves to the beginnings of the struggle for black emancipation from slavery. Hawthorne's comments on Story's rendering of Cleopatra's physical appearance in marble reflect the fashion for orientalism among nineteenth-century western writers, artists and travellers who had become fascinated with the Levant and North Africa:

> The sculptor had not shunned to give the full Nubian lips, and other characteristics of the Egyptian physiognomy. His courage and integrity had been abundantly rewarded, for Cleopatra's beauty shone out richer, warmer, more

triumphantly beyond comparison, than if, shrinking timidly
from the truth, he had chosen the tame Grecian type.

Hawthorne, *The Marble Faun,* 1860
(reprinted London 1995, 2000)

These newly accessible regions were seen as exotic and sensual
landscapes in which to indulge desires that could not be
realised in attractive circumstances in strait-laced nineteenth-
century western society. Western reactions to the oriental
nirvana were naturally coloured by the circumstances of the
artist's home country. Thus in the context of the American
Civil War, Hawthorne, Story and others created their orientalist vision of Cleopatra for positive and progressive reasons:
they intended to advance the cause of an oppressed minority
by offering them a powerful icon of female leadership. Story
had convinced himself of Cleopatra's Egyptian genealogy, and
contemporary critics were generous with praise of his motives
if less respectful of his scholarship:

> We may ethnographically object that Cleopatra, sprung
> from Hellenic blood, could not be African in type. Still it is
> a generous idea, growing out of the spirit of the age – the
> uplifting of downtrodden races to an equality of chances in
> life with the most favored to bestow upon one of Africa's
> daughters the possibility of the intellectual powers and
> physical attraction of the Greek siren.
>
> James Jackson Jarves, reprinted in B. Rowland (ed.),
> *The Art Idea* (Cambridge 1960).

James Jackson Jarves (1818-88), hugely influential in his day as
a critic and collector, enjoyed an exceptionally wide-ranging

career, from founding a newspaper in Hawaii to serving as American vice-consul in Florence. In stark contrast to his liberal views, the nineteenth-century western European orientalist awarded Cleopatra her ancient Roman identity as a dusky oriental temptress. At the turn of the eighteenth and nineteenth centuries, the exploration and documentation of ancient and contemporary Egypt, systematically undertaken for the first time by Napoleon's forces, excited western interest in the imagined exotic and erotic nature of the country. The sensual reaction to Napoleon's vision of Egypt is reflected in nineteenth-century images and literary descriptions – many enthusiastic in their endorsement – of Cleopatra as a sexual enchantress.

However, many persons of influence in the west proclaimed the values of personal chastity and military valour urged on his subjects by Cleopatra's Roman enemy Octavian. Napoleon himself imitated Octavian's personal appearance as it was known from surviving coins and statues. A dual characterisation of Cleopatra thereby emerged, some writers and artists offering interpretations of the queen's character as dark as any devised in ancient Rome, having absorbed the Roman view of her emotional greed, depravity and gluttonous behaviour. The ancient sources were embroidered to suit the tastes of a nineteenth-century western audience, though it must be said that, when it came to describing Cleopatra's world, Roman authors had their own agendas and appear to offer every licence for embellishment. The Roman satirist Lucan, for example, offers a splendid picture of Cleopatra's apartments in which Caesar was to be entertained, the point of the story being that the great man was immune to the queen's wealth and personal charm, preferring instead to spend the night in intellectual discourse about the Nile and its flood:

> Great was the bustle as Cleopatra displayed
> a magnificence not yet adopted in Roman ways.
> A temple-sized hall, too costly for an age
> corrupted with pleasure-spending. The ceiling-panels
> blazed wealth, the rafters hidden in thick gold.
> Marble the walls shone, not with mere veneers,
> agate in its own right, not just decoration,
> and porphyry; on alabaster they trod
> throughout the hall. Meroe's ebony
> replaced mere wood, not a thin cover of doors;
> structural, not for a show. The porch was ivory;
> Indian tortoise-shell, hand-coloured, stood,
> inlaying doors, with emeralds in its spots.
> Gem-gleamed the couches, jasper-tawny cups
> loaded the tables, the sofas bright with hues
> of coverlets, mostly steeped in Tyrian [purple] dye
> of many soakings, others richly embroidered
> with gold or fiery scarlet in the way
> Egyptians mingle leashes in the web.
>
> Lucan, *Civil War* 109ff., trans. Jack Lindsay

Transformed by the pen of Théophile Gautier, *One of Cleopatra's Nights and Other Fantastic Romances* (1838, translated by Lafcadio Hearn), the luxurious setting becomes a corrupting nightmare in which Cleopatra's servant lover 'Monkey' will shortly lose his life:

> Meiamoun, whose head was resting on Cleopatra's shoulder, felt as though his reason was leaving him. The banquet-hall

whirled around him like a vast architectural nightmare; through the dizzy glare he beheld perspectives and colonnades without end; new zones of porticoes seemed to uprear themselves upon the real fabric, and bury their summits in heights of sky to which Babel never rose ....

A similar distortion is applied to the food:

The orgy was at its height: the dishes of flamingoes' tongues, and the livers of *scarus* fish; the eels fattened upon human flesh, and cooked in brine; the dishes of peacocks' brains; the boars stuffed with live birds, and all the marvels of the antique banquets were heaped upon the three table-surfaces of the gigantic triclinium. The wines of Crete, of Massicus and Falernus foamed up in cratera wreathed with roses, and filled by Asian pages whose beautiful flowing hair served the guests to wipe their hands on ....

In contrast, Lucan, *Civil War* X (quoted below) spares none of the theatrical glamour but also commends the care spent on the maturing of the wine and the transport of the oils of cinnamon and cardamom, expertise wholly lacking from the vision offered by Gautier (above), which appears all the more grotesque for its excruciating detail.

Every variety of flesh, fowl, sea-fish or river-fish, every delicacy that extravagance, prompted not by hunger but by a mad love of ostentation, could rout out from the ends of the earth, came served on golden dishes. Cleopatra went so far as to offer Caesar birds and beasts which the Egyptians held sacred; and provided Nile water in ewers of rock crystal for washing his hands. The wine in those huge jewelled goblets was of no local vintage, but a Falernian fetched from Italy, which though a little rough when first casked, becomes nobly mellowed after a few years of careful cellarage at Meroe in Upper Egypt. Each guest had received wreaths of flowering spikenard and perpetual roses, and the fresh oil of cinnamon which they poured on their hair had lost none of its fragrance in transit from the east; and to this they added oil of cardamom recently imported.

A little further on in Gautier's vision of Cleopatra's night, Meiamoun becomes a victim of Cleopatra, who poisons him with boiling, hissing venom delivered from a horn borne by 'an Ethiopian slave of sinister countenance'. As Meiamoun dies in the queen's arms, Antony arrives and queries the corpse, now languishing upon the pavement. 'Oh, nothing,' replies Cleopatra, with a smile; 'only the poison I was testing with the idea of using it on myself should Augustus take me prisoner. My dear Lord, won't you please take a seat by me, and watch those Greek buffoons dance?'

The poisoning of Cleopatra's servants or prisoners was a subject that appealed greatly to orientalist artists, regardless of gender: thus in a canvas by Suzanne Daynes-Grassot, Cleopatra reclines half-naked on a bed in an adjacent room watching three naked female slaves writhe in agony in the foreground, the sinister black poisoner marching off to the left. Another huge canvas painted by Alexandre Cabanel in 1887 (Plate 2) has Cleopatra reclining on a raised dais in slightly somnolent authority, fanned by a half-naked maid, a pet leopard beside her. The women watch as a dead male prisoner is removed, while another collapses before the woman who has brought the poison.

In each of these examples, the victims' gender or identity is changed, as is the setting, in an attempt to 'sex up' the story. The anonymous ancient source of this story has Cleopatra coldly scrutinising the agonies of condemned men in the market place as she tests various poisons before settling upon the asp-bite, considered in Alexandria a relatively humane form of execution.

The fantastical imaginings of orientalist painters, often themselves working to epic scale, nourished the roots of twentieth-century epic cinema: it is this ultimately negative if titillating tradition that was to produce Theda Bara, herself an exotic invention who played Cleopatra as vamp (Fox Studios 1917), and, nearly half a century later, Miss Taylor's interpretation, among many less memorable productions. Cecil B. DeMille's film of 1934, starring Claudette Colbert, was an altogether more sophisticated reading of its multifaceted royal subject, drawing on earlier western tradition. The story of Antony and Cleopatra wrought seductive magic on the actors: in their joint appearances in the Shaw and Shakespeare plays in London and New York in 1951, Vivien Leigh and Laurence Olivier foreshadowed the fabled off-screen romance between Elizabeth Taylor and her co-star Richard Burton.

Earlier European images of Cleopatra

Indeed, before Egypt was explored, offering the opportunity to restore her to an exotic setting, Cleopatra had appeared in western European art and literature as a white-skinned

European princess, mocked for her extravagance yet admired for her integrity in choosing suicide over submission to Octavian. The transformation of the flighty, indulgent princess into a steely, tragic heroine is the subject of Shakespeare's famous tragedy *Antony and Cleopatra* (1608); a more focused exploration of the emotional drama is the meat of John Dryden's play *All for Love* (1678), more popular in its day than Shakespeare's enduring epic vision. The exemplary nature of that momentous moral journey surely explains why two apparently contradictory scenes, one portraying Cleopatra's extravagant competitive banquet with Antony, as recorded by the Roman encyclopaedist the elder Pliny, the other her noble suicide, as recounted by Plutarch, often appear together, especially in pre-orientalist European art. These were by far the most popular choices for representations of the queen, and they were made in a remarkable range of formats. On the grand scale were the murals designed for villas and palaces such as the Palazzo Labia in Venice (the work of the eighteenth-century painter Giambattista Tiepolo), or Burghley House in Lincolnshire, England, where the principal staircase of an imposing Elizabethan fortified residence was in the eighteenth century decorated by Thomas Stothard with images of the Egyptian queen. These mural paintings are reminiscent of sets for theatrical and operatic productions, of which many told the tale of Cleopatra. In the collections of Burghley House may also be found an evocative painting by the eighteenth-century Swiss artist Angelika Kauffmann of Cleopatra mourning at Antony's tomb (cover picture), a scene recounted with some tenderness by Plutarch.

The suicidal Cleopatra appears, to the modern eye unexpectedly, on objects of intimate daily use and interior
adornment, such as pocket-watches or porcelain vases. The
luxurious seventeenth-century pocket-watches made in
London were even faked on the continent. Italian Renaissance
cameos of Cleopatra applying the asp to her breast, her hair
elaborately dressed in contemporary fashion, apparently
allowed aristocratic women to compare their integrity in love
with that of the Egyptian queen (Plate 3).

Early Renaissance manuscript illuminations of texts such
as Boccaccio's *Lives of Famous Men* and *Lives of Famous
Women*, or French or Latin translations of Plutarch's *Parallel
Lives,* offer a rich source of such images: sometimes the
suicides of Antony and Cleopatra were conflated to dramatise
the tragedy, incongruously set in a north-western European
landscape. Some of these exquisite miniatures (often prepared
for practical reasons having to do with the composition of the
book) illustrated other poignant moments in the story, such
as the unsuccessful plea for mercy to Octavian's men by
Antyllus, the son of Antony's earlier marriage to Fulvia.
While the Bruges Boccaccio shows Cleopatra dressed as an
extravagant western queen, sporting a horned headdress
widely condemned at the time for its ostentation and
applying the asps to her exposed breasts, another painting,
recorded in the Royal Library at Windsor by 1542, portrays
an improbably blonde and youthful figure, simply if regally
dressed, standing in a meadow, the blood spurting from the
veins in her arms. It is indeed more likely that the asps were
applied to the arms than the breast, though the more titillating alternative was preferred by the overwhelming majority

of artists. Model for the latter pose was the Vatican 'Cleopatra', an ancient marble sculpture better identified as the Cretan princess Ariadne, and shown in a pose of abandonment, with one arm, suggestively adorned with a bracelet in the form of a snake, crooked behind her head to leave the breast suitably exposed. This imposing figure was displayed by 1520 in the Belvedere of the Vatican, where artists admired it. As late as the 1770s the society painter Pompeo Battoni used the Vatican 'Cleopatra' for an image of Princess of Louise of Brunswick, who lurks in the background of a grand portrait of her young lover Thomas Coke of Holkham, Norfolk. It is said that the princess herself commissioned the portrait, disappointed in her marriage to the ageing and inebriate Bonnie Prince Charlie.

Cleopatra in modern Egypt

In the early 1930s a German team excavating at the eighteenth-dynasty city of Akhetaten (Amarna) discovered what would become the definitive image of Queen Nefertiti. Today the bust, which was in fact a sculptor's model rather than a finished statue, is housed in the Egyptian Museum, Berlin, where it has become an icon of physical beauty and of the irresistible lure of pharaonic Egypt. In contrast only the two-dimensional temple reliefs have been universally accepted as images in the Egyptian style of Cleopatra VII (for the Temple of Hathor at Denderah, see Plate 19; these images are identified by name in the accompanying cartouches), and local admirers of this particular queen have resorted to montages in order to represent her (Plate 4).

Without exception, Cleopatra always appears as an Egyptian, usually borrowing the iconography of Isis, with a vulture headdress representing her divine form. However, the Cleopatra of modern Egypt does not wear the sun disk and cow's horns that distinguish the true Isis, an omission that raises the question of the source of the modern image. It is possible that the design for Cleopatra was invented at some time in the middle of the twentieth century. Before this time, on cigar labels for instance, an exotic orientalist woman figures in an appropriate scene – she can often be found languishing on a couch. In contrast, the modern Cleopatra has more in common with a nineteenth-century pastiche drawing of a temple relief. The inspiration for this figure can be clearly found at Denderah, but, instead of copying the queen's representation on the south wall of the shrine, the artist has selected one of the seated figures of Isis, probably from the crypts. This image shows a representation of the goddess Isis, with vulture headdress and the usual crown (sun disk and cow's horns), and with the hieroglyph of a throne sign spelling her name on top of the disk in a manner sometimes, but not always, used in ancient Egyptian reliefs. The queen is identified by a cartouche that spells the name 'Cleopatra' in a hieroglyphic Egyptian text.

The montage is itself of considerable interest, not least because there is only one surviving ancient statue of Cleopatra in the form of Isis, until recently unidentified. The creator, clearly aware of the queen's association with the goddess, chose to use the attributes of Isis but to leave no doubt over the identity of the queen – hence the cartouche spelling of her name was added. It has even been suggested that the drawing sparked a number of forgeries and the addition of a modern cartouche to an ancient statue that is now in the Metropolitan Museum of Art, New York (Plate 5). A postcard of the pastiche can still be bought today. The description states that it is a representation of Cleopatra from Denderah temple.

In Egypt today this hybrid image is most commonly found on the national brand of cigarettes, albeit in adapted form (Plate 4). The format has thus been transferred to the tourist market. If you ask for a 'Cleopatra' in the souk you will be presented with an image that shows a young female wearing the vulture headdress and head, with a tripartite Egyptian wig and pectoral (breast plate); the crown is optional. On some hand-crafted wooden figures, Cleopatra and Isis maintain their distinct identities. Isis is shown with the 'correct' crown and Cleopatra, interestingly, is shown wearing a crown composed of a sun disk and cow's horns but with additional double plumes. This was the crown that Cleopatra most commonly wore, drawing on the evidence of the temple reliefs (Plate 19) and possibly one of her statues (p. 107). In drawings created for popular use, such as cigarette packets, a snake often mischievously dangles from her ear in profile, copying the Amarna reliefs of Nefertiti. In the case of Cleopatra, however, the snake potentially has a double meaning: to protect her as the uraeus (royal cobra) or to refer to her death.

In addition to appearing on Egyptian cigarettes, Cleopatra's name and image are widely used for such diverse brands as hotels, incense, a tram-stop, a train station in Alexandria and indeed an entire area of the north-east of the city. On the Egyptian wine 'Cru des Ptolémées', it is the queen's image that decorates the label, no doubt an association that Cleopatra would have approved if the stories of her revelries are to be believed. In the logo of Banque Misr, Egypt's national bank, the same bust appears: here, the modern image of Cleopatra seems to represent 'Egypt' itself. On each occasion the image evokes the queen's Egyptian identity, and indeed the archaeo-logical evidence suggests that this is how the queen intended herself to be seen in her home country. Cleopatra thus quite literally remains an Egyptian national treasure. The name 'Cleopatra' is not needed for these national representations and in no case does it appear in ancient Egyptian hieroglyphic script. In most cases no name accompanies the representations of Cleopatra made for the tourist market. The same is true of Nefertiti. On some imported items such as Cleopatra mugs, most of which are nowadays made in China, nonsense hiero-glyphs surround the queen's recognisable image, and she is accompanied by a fictitious cartouche. On some the name 'Cleopatra' appears; written in Roman script, for only a non-Egyptian is deemed to need this prompt.

All these Cleopatras are of considerable interest in exploring the attitudes various societies have taken towards one of the most charismatic figures of history, using the last queen of Egypt to mirror their sexual desires, and their social and political aspirations, along with their fears. The extraor-dinarily varied nature of the depictions of the queen reflects her unique stature in her own world. Here was a woman ruler who threatened invincible Rome with her wealth and personal power. This last quality Cleopatra had in spades, not only by virtue of her royal authority but also as a result of her own considerable intellect and character. However hostile they may have been to her political aspirations, the ancient sources agree that Cleopatra was a person of intelligence, wit and enormous, irresistible charisma. As to her physical beauty, a topic of continuing interest in the modern world, they are at most equivocal. Plutarch speaks of her exquisite, mesmerising voice, a quality of enormous importance to a politician as to a lover, and one often underrated by a modern public accustomed to the dominance of visual images. Ancient visual images of Cleopatra appear to have been tailored to suit their use: these are explored in greater detail on pp. 70-95.

2

The Historical Cleopatra

As we have seen, over the two millennia that have passed since her death, Cleopatra's identity has been adjusted to fit the aspirations of a remarkable range of cultures. The unusual malleability of Cleopatra's identity reflects both the queen's importance as an historical figure and the relative lack of hard information about her from contemporary sources. Here follows a brief review of the historical background to the emergence of Cleopatra, last queen of independent Egypt and last of the Ptolemaic dynasty. A condensed family tree of the Ptolemies is given on pp. 30-1 (Fig. 1).

The Ptolemies

Each Ptolemaic king was named after Ptolemy son of Lagos, the first king of the line – indeed, the Ptolemies are some-times known as the Lagids. Individual kings were distinguished by flattering epithets describing their character or achievement: some later Ptolemies were given rather less desirable epithets by their irreverent Alexandrian subjects. Thus the first Ptolemy was known as Soter (the saviour), the second Philadelphus (lover of his sister – or brother) and the third Euergetes (the benefactor). The eighth Ptolemy was also called Euergetes but was nicknamed by his subjects Physcon

(Fatty or Pot-belly) for what would today be termed an obesity problem.

Of Macedonian Greek origin, the first Ptolemy had fought with distinction as a senior commander in the army of the legendary Macedonian king Alexander the Great. When in 323 BC Alexander died of a fever at Babylon in Mesopotamia (now Iraq), Ptolemy diverted the young king's body from Syria, where the cortège had reached on its way to burial in Macedonia, and brought it to Egypt. Taking Alexander's corpse first to the royal city of Memphis, he eventually buried it in the newly founded city of Alexandria. Named for its founder Alexander, the city was built, principally for economic reasons, on the Mediterranean coast to the west of the Nile Delta. Under the patronage of the early Ptolemies, Alexandria became the intellectual and artistic centre of the Mediterranean, the very embodiment of what came to be seen by later generations as Alexander's cultural mission. His tomb has yet to be located within the city, which has been densely occupied from its foundation to modern times.

Alexander's empire was divided among his generals: Ptolemy thus took charge of Egypt, first on the lines agreed at the time of Alexander's death, then establishing himself in 305 BC as king in the tradition of Alexander, even using his master's portraits on his coinage to legitimise his own position. Ptolemy's fractious, often dramatically dysfunctional family was to rule Egypt until Cleopatra's defeat by the Roman leader Octavian in 30 BC.

The Ptolemaic period is traditionally separated by historians into three unequally spaced phases: the earliest comprises the reigns of Ptolemies I-III who ruled as kings

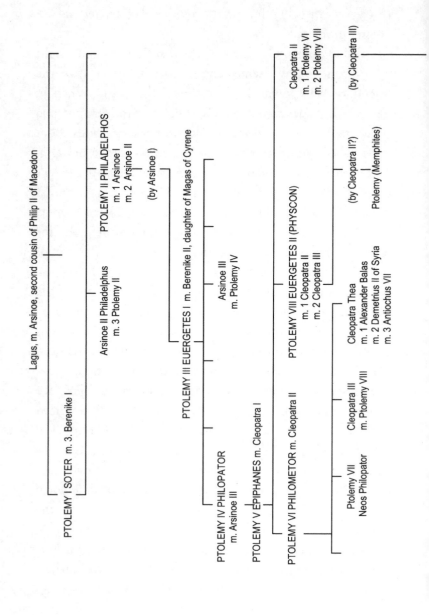

Lagus, m. Arsinoe, second cousin of Philip II of Macedon

PTOLEMY I SOTER m. 3. Berenike I

PTOLEMY II PHILADELPHOS
m. 1 Arsinoe I
m. 2 Arsinoe II

(by Arsinoe I)

Arsinoe II Philadelphus
m. 3 Ptolemy II

PTOLEMY III EUERGETES I m. Berenike II, daughter of Magas of Cyrene

Arsinoe III
m. Ptolemy IV

PTOLEMY IV PHILOPATOR
m. Arsinoe III

PTOLEMY V EPIPHANES m. Cleopatra I

PTOLEMY VI PHILOMETOR m. Cleopatra II

Ptolemy VII
Neos Philopator

Cleopatra III
m. Ptolemy VIII

PTOLEMY VIII EUERGETES II (PHYSCON)
m. 1 Cleopatra II
m. 2 Cleopatra III

Cleopatra Thea
m. 1 Alexander Balas
m. 2 Demetrius II of Syria
m. 3 Antiochus VII

Cleopatra II
m. 1 Ptolemy VI
m. 2 Ptolemy VIII

(by Cleopatra II?)

(by Cleopatra II)
Ptolemy (Memphites)

(by Cleopatra III)

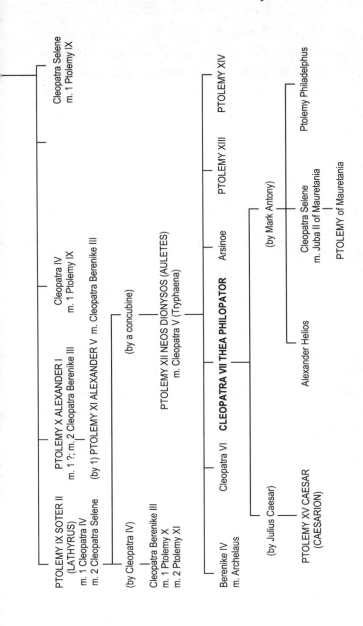

1. Family tree of the Ptolemies.

31

from 305-221 BC. During this time Egypt was at its most prosperous, enjoying the revenues accruing from a substantial number of possessions overseas. A second, more problematic period is placed within the reign of Ptolemy IV Philopator (father-loving: 221-204 BC), whose licentious behaviour, at least according to the second-century BC Greek writer Polybios and other later historians, caused a critical weakening in royal power. While it is certainly true that the fourth Ptolemy enjoyed a personal association with the Greek god of wine Dionysos, and a lifestyle to match it, modern historians have been kinder in their interpretation of this ruler's capabilities. This reign is symptomatic of what would become the norm in the last phase of Ptolemaic rule, from Ptolemy IV's death in 204 BC to the dynasty's fall with Cleopatra's suicide in 30 BC: rebellions, disputes and wars about foreign possessions, and, most dangerously, pretenders to the throne, in this instance arising from native rebels in the south of Egypt. However, that Ptolemy IV was the first to include native Egyptian troops in the Egyptian army, rather than Greek mercenaries, might now be interpreted as a positive move, an acknowledgement of acculturation rather than a sign of weakness and indeed imminent downfall, as expressed in the somewhat colonialist attitude of earlier modern historians. The fact that the rulers of the second century BC appear more frequently in Egyptian-style temple reliefs and free-standing statuary suggests that their embrace of Egypt's culture and its people was part of a more general and, one might argue, a natural progression as the Ptolemies became entrenched in Egypt's long history and distinctive character.

Nonetheless, the legacy that Ptolemy IV left to his six-year-old son did not bode well for the dynasty's future. Soon after the death of his father in 204 BC Ptolemy V Epiphanes (the god made manifest) found himself doubly orphaned, his mother Arsinoe III murdered by a royal advisor who wished to enhance his own position. When the young king came of age, the royal court was moved to the traditional capital of Memphis, perhaps to forget the bloodshed of the palaces in Alexandria. It seems that Ptolemy V lived by Ptolemaic royal standards a relatively quiet life; it was in fact his Syrian wife Cleopatra I who became one of the first queens to hold real power, both in her own right and as regent to her son, Ptolemy VI.

Ptolemaic queens

Unlike her predecessors Berenike II, wife of Ptolemy III, and Arsinoe III, the long-suffering wife of Ptolemy IV, the first Cleopatra survived her husband's death, and in many respects created roles for herself that elevated her in a manner suited to the mother of the pharaoh, following earlier Egyptian tradition. Thus Cleopatra I was made a goddess during her lifetime and celebrated her status by minting coins in her own right; she accompanied her son on his royal duties and took the title *thea* (goddess). Though some scholars have made the case for Arsinoe II, the surviving evidence strongly suggests that individual deification in life had not been achieved by any earlier Ptolemaic queen, and was only won by Cleopatra I through the revival of dynastic Egyptian roles relating to her status as the king's mother. Berenike I had been deified posthumously along with her husband Ptolemy I, while Arsinoe II, Berenike II and Arsinoe III had only been allocated their own cults and priestesses following their deaths. Cleopatra's innovation was therefore a breakthrough for Ptolemaic royal women, giving them as a group greater autonomy and power.

It is interesting to note that, as the Ptolemies grew weaker on the international political scene and more dependent upon Rome, the queens started to obtain greater real political power of their own. Cleopatra I produced arguably the most problematic siblings of the entire dynasty, including a daughter, Cleopatra II, who was to elevate herself to ruler at the expense of her second husband and brother Ptolemy VIII. This king had killed his own nephew Ptolemy VII, the younger son of Cleopatra II by her first husband and other brother Ptolemy VI, in order to seize control of the throne. He then married the mother of his murdered relative, his sister Cleopatra II. In the second Cleopatra we find a ruthless woman willing to compromise her integrity in order to remain in power. This is illustrated nowhere better than in the fate of her second child, Ptolemy Memphites, of whom Ptolemy VIII was the father. The young boy was lured to Cyprus, where his father lived in exile with his second wife, his niece Cleopatra III, daughter of Ptolemy VI and Cleopatra II; the child was killed in 132/1 BC, dismembered and delivered to Cleopatra II at her birthday feast as a reminder that the rightful ruler was not happy to have been usurped. Despite this violent turn of events, the three contenders for power (that is, Ptolemy VIII and Cleopatras II and III) were reconciled to rule Egypt together once again.

Both Cleopatra II and her daughter Cleopatra III, the second wife of Ptolemy VIII, survived their husband, a man who had obtained little respect from his Alexandrian subjects, as his nickname 'Physcon' ('Fatty') shows. However, the actions of these two women paved the way for Cleopatra VII. Indeed, in order to understand the last Ptolemaic queen, it is helpful to delve into her family history.

Cleopatras II and III had shown that women could rule in their own right, and on occasion could win popularity among their subjects and so power of their own. The stories of Cleopatra II and indeed Cleopatra III, who ruled with her two sons, must have been known to Cleopatra VII, the great-granddaughter of Cleopatra III. The latter queen was murdered by her favourite son, Ptolemy X, in the summer of 101 BC, fifty years before the last Ptolemaic queen came to the throne. Even to a modern viewer, the third Cleopatra's images project a sense of personal power, and the surviving temple reliefs show her taking the lead, often standing before her sons in a dominant position. If the last Cleopatra needed a role model and reminder of just how difficult it was to be a Ptolemaic queen, she need have looked no further.

The treachery of men, however, was even closer to the last queen's immediate past. Cleopatra Berenike III, a daughter of Ptolemy IX, who replaced Cleopatra III as the consort of Ptolemy X, was later married off to her stepson, Ptolemy XI, when it had been decided that she should take a new consort. The marriage lasted no more than three weeks: Cleopatra Berenike III was murdered by her husband. He had already been confirmed as king by the Romans, who by the end of the second century BC were masters of the Mediterranean world and taking a keen interest in the rule of its richest country, Egypt. But then in true patriotic style the Alexandrians murdered the royal assailant of their popular queen. Cleopatra

VII's father, an illegitimate son of Ptolemy IX, was summoned to take the throne in place of the dead couple and it seems that, with the exception of her father Ptolemy XII, Cleopatra was understandably wary of the men in her life.

Cleopatra and her immediate family

The last ruler of independent Egypt is commonly referred to as the seventh of the Ptolemaic queens to bear the name Cleopatra, a royal Macedonian Greek name meaning 'father-honouring'. The sense of closeness with her father is further emphasised in Cleopatra's epithet 'father-loving', used in both her Greek and Egyptian titles. It was perhaps a reflection of genuine sentiment, as Cleopatra was evidently very close to her father, Ptolemy XII Theos Philopator Philadelphus Neos Dionysos (the God, Father-loving, Brother-loving, the New Dionysos). Continuing the recently established Ptolemaic tradition of taking the name of a god, he was mocked by his subjects with the nickname Auletes (the Flute Player) for his preference for extravagant Dionysiac entertainment over matters of state.

There is some argument among scholars over whether Cleopatra's mother was Ptolemy XII's first consort, his sister the fifth Cleopatra Tryphaena (the Bountiful), who disappeared from the record by 68 BC, and considerably more uncertainty over the identity, personal and ethnic, of her paternal grandmother, the concubine of Ptolemy IX Soter (Saviour), himself nicknamed 'Lathyros' ('Chickpea'). Indeed, the latter uncertainty gave rise to another nickname for Cleopatra's father: 'Nothos' ('Bastard'). These uncertainties have created room for speculation ancient and modern on Cleopatra's ethnic identity.

Equally uncertain is Cleopatra VII's year of birth, generally assumed to be 70/69 BC. Nor do we know where she was born: we assume the royal palace at Alexandria. The identity of her first-born son and co-ruler is also doubted, as is his year of birth. He ruled as Ptolemy XV Caesar, and was nicknamed by the Alexandrians 'Caesarion' or 'Little Caesar' in an apparent reference to his likely parentage by the Roman Dictator Julius Caesar in 47 or 44 BC.

A dedication made in Athens by 'a Libyan princess' in honour of one of her ladies-in-waiting suggests that Cleopatra accompanied her father to exile in Rome as a child of about twelve (Fig. 2), the disgrace resulting from the displeasure caused by the unacceptably high taxes imposed upon the Alexandrian people to repay Ptolemy Auletes' debt to his Roman patrons Caesar and Pompey. Having settled this bill, Auletes incurred a second liability on the occasion of his restoration in 55 BC by Aulus

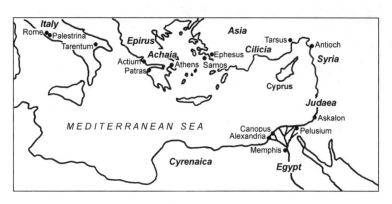

2. *Cleopatra's journeys: map of the central and eastern Mediterranean in Cleopatra's day.*

Gabinius, Roman governor of Syria, whose commander of cavalry was Mark Antony. During the king's period of exile, one of Cleopatra's sisters, Cleopatra VI Tryphaena, had either retired or died; the other, Berenike IV, ruled in her own right, and, after brief marriages to a Syrian prince so coarse he was nicknamed 'Salt-fishmonger' by the Alexandrians, and to Archelaus of Pontus, she and her second husband were deposed and executed. Cleopatra VII then probably co-ruled with her father in the period leading up to his death in 51 BC.

Ptolemy XII had begun his reign in 76 BC. Many of Cleopatra VII's policies and her presentation were influenced by her father's rule, and although during his reign Ptolemy XII accepted a growing dependency on Rome, there is evidence that he also aimed to promote himself strongly in Egypt. Cleopatra seems to have recognised and copied these dual policies, in the latter case strengthening the royal ties with the Egyptian priesthood. Indeed some of the projects started by Ptolemy XII were completed by his daughter.

Like his daughter's reign, and indeed those of his ancestors, Ptolemy XII's reign was chronically unstable, including the period of exile in Rome mentioned above, and the execution of his daughter Berenike IV. Her crime was to have seized control of the throne in her father's absence. Had she bided her time, she might have succeeded her father and the Ptolemaic dynasty might well have died a rather less colourful death than that contrived by Cleopatra VII.

Ptolemy XII's exile was the price of his punitive efforts to prevent Rome from controlling Egypt in the way that the Romans had opportunistically taken control of other Ptolemaic territories. However, in spite of the financial burden of his policy and the glitch in his rule, a large number of temples were under construction or actually dedicated during Ptolemy XII's reign (for the following locations, see Fig. 3). Significantly, the

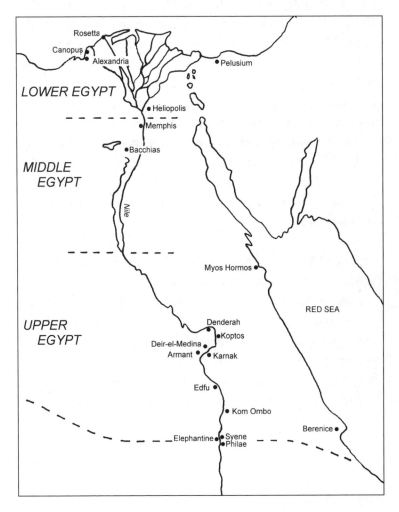

3. *Map of Egypt showing sites associated with Cleopatra.*

majority were in Upper Egypt, an area traditionally seen to be a threat to the Ptolemaic family, partly because of its physical distance from the capital Alexandria, but also because the family had long-standing close ties with the priests in the royal city of Memphis, located closer to the capital just to the south of the Nile Delta. Curiously, a number of buildings dating to the Thirtieth Dynasty were replaced or rebuilt by Ptolemy XII. This development appears to reverse the policies of earlier Ptolemaic kings that seem to have purposefully linked them with the last native Egyptian dynasty.

At all events, the earlier temple at Denderah, now assumed to be Thirtieth Dynasty in date, was replaced with a new temple, which would be completed by Cleopatra VII. Ptolemy XII also built a gateway in the enclosure wall at Koptos, which is usually dated to the reign of either Nectanebo I (Thirtieth Dynasty) or Ptolemy II. One of the gateways of the small Temple of Ptah at Karnak was completed by Ptolemy XII and another minor project included an enclosure wall for the Temple of Hathor at Deir el-Medina on the West Bank at Thebes. And in the Temple of Isis at Philae, decoration of the first pylon continued. It has also been suggested that work on the Temple at Kom Ombo, including an enclosure wall and new monumental gateway, was undertaken during the reign of Ptolemy XII. One of the most substantial projects during his reign was the expansion of the Temple of Horus at Edfu. Here the enclosure wall was finished and a gateway and pylon were erected; on the walls of the latter is the famous relief showing the king smiting his enemies in the traditional Egyptian manner. In this way, Ptolemy XII literally constructed a presence in the all-important south of Egypt.

His buildings, decorated with images promoting his links with the gods and his personal achievements, allowed Ptolemy XII to promote his willing acceptance of his unplanned promotion to serve as Egypt's king.

Ptolemy XII's reign laid the foundations for Cleopatra's personal philosophy of queenship and the style of her rule. In many respects Egypt was powerless. It had become more dependent upon Rome, and its overseas territories had mostly been lost to its European 'ally'. In such circumstances it is entirely understandable that the last Ptolemies should seek to consolidate their power throughout Egypt itself through the construction of sacred buildings bearing flattering regal images and texts.

Ptolemy XII's will is recorded in the Roman sources, and from this point onwards at least those events of Cleopatra's tumultuous 21-year reign that impinge on Rome are well known, though the record is of course coloured by hostile Roman bias. Her father's wish was that the seventeen-year-old Cleopatra should co-rule in traditional style with her younger brother Ptolemy XIII, an arrangement that unfortunately allowed much scope for intrigue by courtiers and advisers who rightly judged the boy more open to manipulation than his highly intelligent and astute elder sister. By 48 BC Cleopatra was ousted, and was only reinstated by a clever and typically theatrical stratagem aimed at winning to her cause the Roman general Julius Caesar.

Cleopatra and Caesar

Caesar was by 48 BC temporarily stationed in the royal palace at Alexandria, in pursuit of Pompey the Great, his opponent in the civil war. Seeking to please the Roman leader, Ptolemy XIII's men ambushed Pompey as he landed on the Egyptian coast at Pelusium. They brought his severed head on a plate to Caesar – a miscalculation, for the Roman leader was mortified and angered by his rival's undignified and un-Roman fate. Cleopatra, hearing of Caesar's displeasure and his intention to fulfil the terms of her father's will, had herself smuggled into the royal palace at Alexandria within a bedroll (later glamorised as an oriental carpet) supplied by a Sicilian merchant named Apollodorus. The scene in which the beautiful young princess emerged from the bedroll to astound Caesar, engaged at the time in writing his military memoirs, has been immortalised in drama, art and film (Plate 6).

Caesar sought to reinstate both rulers on the terms of their father Ptolemy XII's will, but a significant faction in Alexandria, led by Ptolemy XIII's advisor Pothinus, put it about that Caesar planned for his lover Cleopatra to rule alone. War ensued, and, surprised from behind by Pothinus' men, Caesar had to swim for his life in heavy armour (holding aloft his papers) across Alexandria's Great Harbour. It is said that in another dramatic incident the famous library established by the early Ptolemies was destroyed by fire. As in all wars there were moments of extreme uncertainty, but the eventual outcome was predictable: Ptolemy XIII drowned in gilded armour in a skirmish in the Nile Delta, and was succeeded by his younger brother Ptolemy XIV, who was married to Cleopatra on Caesar's orders. Brother and sister were thereby restored to the throne according to the terms of their father's will.

2. The Historical Cleopatra

Cleopatra's surviving sister Arsinoe, who had taken advantage of anti-Roman feeling in Alexandria by allying herself to the Egyptian side, was captured and two years later paraded in Caesar's triumph at Rome. Though there was no love lost between the sisters, it was said that Cleopatra was so distressed by the sight of Arsinoe as the publicly paraded prisoner of the Romans that she vowed never to suffer the same humiliation herself.

Caesar was highly susceptible to the charms of women, notably those of non-Roman royal stock. The voyage of Caesar and Cleopatra up the Nile has become, like the smuggled carpet, the stuff of romantic legend. In fact we do not know how far they travelled, and, far from being a lovers' cruise, the voyage evidently provided an opportunity to display military force, for the royal barge was accompanied by a large number of Caesar's troops. To anyone watching the couple and their entourage, there could be no doubt as to who was now charged with the rule of Egypt. Indeed, to protect his client-queen, Caesar left three legions in Egypt while he moved on to another battlefield – and another royal liaison.

By 46 BC the throne of Egypt was sufficiently secured by Roman forces for Cleopatra to travel to Rome with a large entourage (Fig. 4). She aimed to secure a formal treaty of friendship with the Roman people, and was warmly received by Caesar, who installed her in a villa discreetly located across the Tiber. Certain surviving portraits on gravestones, along with Egyptian cult images and other religious apparatus, suggest considerable local fascination with the Egyptian queen. However, some Romans – notably and most volubly the republican orator Cicero – evidently loathed her.

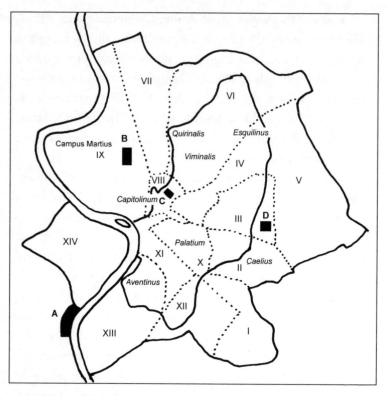

4. Map of Rome showing sites relevant to the story of Cleopatra.

A Caesar's villa, where Cleopatra stayed from 46-44 bc.
B Temple of Isis and Serapis in the Campus Martius, begun by Octavian after Caesar's murder, later destroyed by him but redeveloped by Antony's descendant Gaius (Caligula).
C Temple of Venus Genetrix and Forum of Caesar, where Cleopatra's statue was displayed into late antiquity.
D Temple of Isis and Serapis on the Esquiline Hill, where the head of Cleopatra as Isis was found. The district (III) was called Isis and Serapis.

Cleopatra stayed for two years, apparently under the continued protection – or indeed at the insistence – of Caesar, who commissioned a gilded statue of her to stand in the Temple of Venus Genetrix in his new forum in the centre of Rome (Fig. 4). This extraordinary honour conferred upon Cleopatra equal status with the Roman goddess Venus, legendary mother of Caesar's family. Though it was long-established practice in Egypt for Ptolemaic rulers to share temples with the gods, by whose divine authority they ruled, such an arrangement was then unknown in Rome. To many Romans it would have seemed that by this act Caesar was recognising his son by Cleopatra, if indeed he had been born as many believe in 47 BC. However, Caesar's own aspirations to sole rule by divine authority were opposed by significant factions in Rome, and his liaison with Cleopatra, openly celebrated in the city despite his continued marriage to his Roman wife Calpurnia, would have done nothing to quell suspicion. Indeed, it was the perceived oriental aspect of Caesar's rule as Dictator, magnified by Cleopatra's prolonged presence in Rome with members of her court, which led to his assassination by Brutus and Cassius in March of 44 BC.

No public recognition was made in Caesar's will of Cleopatra's son, and some scholars believe that he was not yet born at the time of the murder. In the immediate wake of this catastrophe, Cleopatra fled Rome for Egypt, her infant son becoming her co-ruler some time after the convenient demise of her second husband and brother Ptolemy XIV from a mysterious illness – interpreted by many as murder – contracted immediately on his return.

Back in Egypt, Cleopatra resumed her commitment to the country, its people and its gods. A number of surviving documents reveal the queen as actively concerned for all her subjects, regardless of religious affiliation or ethnic origin, in difficult years of famine and flood. She also took steps to promote the infant Caesarion as a future senior ruler. The evidence comes from visual and textual sources in Egyptian contexts, as Caesarion was to be assassinated by Octavian's men in the wake of the Roman capture of Alexandria in 30 BC. It is very likely that Caesarion, by right of his mixed Roman and Ptolemaic parentage, was seen by Cleopatra as a royal heir able to work with Rome for the future of an independent Egypt. Rome had intervened in Egyptian affairs for over a century and Cleopatra certainly possessed the vision, the understanding, the experience and the personal connections to see how the difficult relationship might develop to Egypt's advantage in the short- to medium-term future.

Cleopatra and Antony

However, any plans of Cleopatra to develop the dynasty through the agency of her son were interrupted in 41 BC by a summons to a meeting with the Roman general Mark Antony at Tarsus in south-east Asia Minor (see p. 37, Fig. 2). Antony wished to explore options of material support from Cleopatra for his campaigns in Armenia, Parthia and Mesopotamia. Rightly viewing Cleopatra as a pragmatic and politically responsive monarch, he was uncertain of her loyalty. As she had so successfully won the support of Caesar seven years previously, Cleopatra decided on theatre as her best chance of surprising and winning over the distinguished Roman general, who, like Caesar, was widely known to be susceptible to the charms of women. Antony, moreover, was known to be very partial to wine.

2. The Historical Cleopatra

The scene of their meeting on the banks of the river Cydnus was described at some length by Antony's biographer Plutarch, a Greek intellectual writing well over a century after the events. Fourteen centuries later, Plutarch's account was brilliantly reshaped by Shakespeare.

> The barge she sat in, like a burnish'd throne,
> Burned on the water; the poop was beaten gold,
> Purple the sails, and so perfumed that
> The winds were love-sick with them; the oars were silver
> Which to the tune of flutes kept stroke and made
> The water which they beat to follow faster,
> As amorous of their strokes. For her own person
> It beggared all description; she did lie
> In her pavilion, cloth-of-gold, of tissue,
> O'er-picturing that Venus where we see
> The fancy outwork nature; on each side her
> Stood pretty dimpled boys, like smiling Cupids,
> With divers-coloured fans, whose wind did seem
> To glow the delicate cheeks which they did cool,
> And what they undid did …
>   … At the helm
> A seeming mermaid steers: the silken tackle
> Swell with the touches of those flower-soft hands,
> That yarely frame the office. From the barge
> A strange invisible perfume hits the sense
> Of the adjacent wharfs. The city cast
> Her people out on her; and Antony,
> Enthroned i' th' market-place, did sit alone,
> Whistling to the th' air: which but for vacancy,
> Had gone to gaze on Cleopatra too,
> And made a gap in nature.

Antony was enraptured, and awed by the sumptuous splendour of the feasts and gifts offered to him and his men by Cleopatra, and not least by the lighting arrangements, a detail noted by Plutarch which adds to the sense of dramatic display. Their relationship was to remain highly competitive, each vying with the other to outdo their efforts at consumption, whether of food, wine, sex, money, ships, palaces, jewels, even fish to be caught in Alexandria harbour. The modern catchphrase 'bling bling' might have been invented for Antony and Cleopatra: they called themselves 'The Society of Inimitable Livers', with characteristic wit changing the name to 'Those who are going to die together' when their fate was eventually sealed. A wit in Alexandria, probably one of Antony's dependants, given his name 'Parasite', described Antony as 'the inimitable lover'. The text appears on a statue base, but unfortunately the statue has not survived.

Antony was put under enormous pressure to come to his Roman senses and make his peace with his powerful rival Octavian, the much younger Roman heir to Caesar's name and fortune, who later became the first Roman emperor Augustus. Antony chose to do so by abandoning Cleopatra in 40 BC for marriage at Rome to Octavian's sister Octavia. In the same year Cleopatra gave birth to twins, Alexander and Cleopatra, later named Helios and Selene (the Sun and the Moon). After only three years, in which Octavia bore Antony two daughters, both named after him, Antony returned to Alexandria, and thereafter remained with Cleopatra until their deaths. Cleopatra gave birth to a son named Ptolemaios the year after his return.

By then, Antony had resumed his plans for building his

empire in the east, campaigning in Parthia, Mesopotamia and Armenia. He was able to call once more upon the enormous resources of Cleopatra, and their liaison was celebrated on silver and bronze coins of various denominations, some minted in cities given to Cleopatra by Antony on his return, others at unknown sites, from 37 to the final showdown with Octavian at Actium in 31 BC. The coins (Plate 7) displayed images of the two rulers, on most examples occupying one side each, with Cleopatra assuming eastern dress, along with oriental appearance and the royal title 'Queen Cleopatra Thea II'. The meaning of the title is disputed, but it most likely reflects the achievements of Cleopatra's notorious great-aunt Cleopatra Thea, who through her marriages to Syrian kings had temporarily gained a similar range of territories perceived as vital to the defence of Egypt (Plate 8). In contrast, Antony remained supreme commander and tribune of the Roman people, the titles directly translated from the Latin, though the mighty aspect of his physique belied the modesty of the legend. Though the coins were inscribed in Greek, the legend was written in the nominative case in Roman fashion. These coins offer a fascinating microcosm of Roman, Greek and Mesopotamian ideas of leadership.

Antony was criticised in Rome for botching these campaigns by mistiming his operations, thereby allowing troops to perish unnecessarily in bad winter weather, and failing to maintain adequate supplies. These uncharacteristic errors were attributed by writers such as Livy to Antony's unseemly haste to return to Cleopatra, who had accustomed him to a soft, Dionysiac urban lifestyle inappropriate to military command.

Any victory in Armenia was actually won in the field of battle by Antony's senior commander Publius Canidius Crassus, and a recently discovered papyrus shows how the queen of Egypt rewarded him within the year with important tax concessions and trading permits. Cleopatra could afford to be generous: the gains from this campaign for the queen and her family were exceptional, with vast swathes of territory across the eastern Mediterranean and far to the east granted to the family along with the grandiose titles (Plate 9, Fig. 5). Cleopatra also received the hugely profitable territory of Gaza and its hinterland, planted with balsam groves.

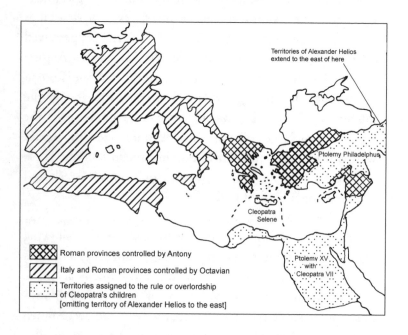

5. Map of the 'Donations of Alexandria'.

News of this remarkable development was rec
mounting alarm in Rome, where a campaign was
discredit Cleopatra, portraying Antony and Octav.   ....er
hapless victims. Cleopatra became a non-person, the embodiment of the un-Roman vice of lack of control of her
appetites, whether gluttonous or sensual. Indeed she came to
represent the powerful threat of the orient with all the over-
tones of excess later to be recaptured in nineteenth-century
romantic orientalism. The hitherto courageous Antony was
in Roman eyes but putty in the hands of the queen whose
persona had taken on the aspect of Methe (drunkenness):
Antony himself wittily riposted with a pamphlet entitled
'On his own drunkenness', the text of which alas has not
survived. In contrast, the abandoned Octavia was heroised
and lauded with public honours. Indeed she behaved with
saintly generosity of spirit, long refusing to leave the marital
home, even raising not only her children by Antony, but
those of Antony's deceased previous wife Fulvia, and eventually even his surviving children by Cleopatra.

In 32 BC Antony and Octavia were formally divorced. As
the hostile climate increased in intensity, Octavian vowed that
'all Italy' supported his campaign against the threat posed by
the queen of Egypt and her Roman victim. In fact Italy was
less united than he claimed: a number of prominent Romans
supported Antony, including the two consuls for 32/31 BC,
Gnaeus Domitius Ahenobarbus and Gaius Sosius, and there is
some evidence that coins were minted in central Italy in
support of Antony and Cleopatra. A dramatic instance of
rapidly changing allegiance is offered by Scarpus, the Roman
governor of Cyrene in Libya, nominally controlled by Antony

and Cleopatra's twin daughter Cleopatra Selene. Here coins for both Cleopatra and Octavian were struck within the year 31/30 BC.

The Battle of Actium and its aftermath

Conflict appeared inevitable, and once more we hear (from Plutarch) of Cleopatra's ally and Antony's right-hand man Publius Canidius. In 31 BC he repaid Cleopatra's generous tax concessions by petitioning Antony on her behalf. Antony did not wish Cleopatra to play a personal role in the battle with Octavian: her ships were too heavy, and a liability in any skirmish with the versatile Roman fleet commanded by Octavian's admiral Marcus Agrippa. Moreover Cleopatra, perhaps with an eye to entering Rome, if not considering the less attractive proposition of defeat and exile from Alexandria, insisted on bringing her entire retinue and treasure with her. She and Antony gathered support en route from the kings and councils of many of the cities of Asia Minor and Greece itself. Patras in the north-western Greek Peloponnese provided their winter quarters, and was also the location of their last celebration, issuing coins with a head of Isis on the reverse.

The engagement took place further north, by Cape Actium, a promontory controlling access to the Gulf of Ambracia (see p. 37, Fig. 2). Antony and Cleopatra's fleets were encircled by Agrippa's lighter ships, but managed to break through the trap. The queen fled, with Antony's fleet following her; they headed south-east to Alexandria. For much of the way they were pursued by Agrippa's fleet, but they succeeded in reaching the sanctuary of the Nile Delta. Octavian himself sailed to Syria, where he summoned Cleopatra to treat with him. She refused to surrender her royal authority or her person.

There then followed distressing episodes worthy of the dramatic tragedy that even today dominates our view of Cleopatra. With Octavian's army at the gates of Alexandria, Antony became depressed, seeing the last revellers from a Dionysiac feast making their way home through the streets, and sensing acutely the end of his festive life with the Queen of Egypt. He heard rumours that Cleopatra, locked in her mausoleum, had committed suicide. Antony threw himself on his sword, fatally wounding but not immediately killing himself. The queen, hearing of this, had Antony brought to her: hoisted to the upper chamber of the mausoleum, he died in her arms.

Octavian may have wished to parade the defeated queen of Egypt in triumph at Rome. He had her watched by his men, but not closely enough. It is indeed possible that her suicide offered a face-saving solution to him. Thus, after extravagant mourning, Cleopatra visited Antony's tomb and offered the traditional eulogy of his many fine qualities. She bathed herself, and dressed in her finest clothes. She then prepared a feast. A country boy arrived with a basket of figs, within which were concealed two asps. These Cleopatra applied to her body (most likely to veins in her arms rather than her breasts, as is so often depicted in Renaissance and later images of her suicide (Plate 3). Octavian's men discovered her dying: they summoned Libyans expert in the treatment of snake venom, but were too late to save her. In the long view of history it was widely agreed that the manner of her death (the asp being related to the Egyptian royal cobra) befitted the last queen of Egypt. Moreover, in her suicide, Cleopatra had showed integrity. She had refused to submit to Octavian, and had remained loyal to Antony, showing him love and respect.

The queen had arranged for her eldest son and co-ruler Caesarion to escape to India via friendly kings in Arabia. However, he made a fatal decision to return to Alexandria from the Red Sea port of Myos Hormos. In the capital he was assassinated by Octavian's men, a fate that also befell Antyllus, Caesarion's exact contemporary and the product of Antony's marriage to Fulvia. Poignantly, both youths had celebrated that very year their entry into adult life: Caesarion followed the Greek rite of entry to the ephebate, the elite group of youths who underwent military, philosophical and athletic training for leadership, while Antyllus put on the Roman *toga virilis*, standard dress for elite adult males. Octavian himself visited Alexandria only briefly. He paid his respects to the mummified corpse of Alexander the Great, famously causing its nose to fall off. He refused to visit the tombs of the Ptolemies, dismissing them as nothing more than cadavers of no interest to the ruler of the known world. In a striking illustration of the modern maxim that today's news wraps tomorrow's fish and chips, the papyrus formally recording Cleopatra's gifts to Antony's general Canidius was discarded, later to be recycled as wrapping for a Roman mummy buried in the cemeteries at Aboukir, east of Alexandria.

Cleopatra and Antony's surviving children were removed

to Rome where they were paraded in triumph. Octavian had to be content with exhibiting an effigy of Cleopatra, which showed her in the act of suicide by snake-bite. Of the children, we hear more only of Cleopatra Selene, who was married to Juba II of Numidia, and lived a Ptolemaic royal life in all but name at their capital Iol Caesarea (Cherchel in modern Algeria), renamed in honour of Caesar Augustus. Cleopatra Selene died, apparently of natural causes, at the age of 35. Her son, significantly named Ptolemaeus, succeeded his father and ruled until the era of the emperor Claudius, himself descended from Antony through his Roman wife Octavia.

Indeed, under the later Julio-Claudian emperors, Gaius (better known today as Caligula, AD 37-41), Claudius (AD 41-54) and Nero (AD 54-68), the Roman imperial court itself took on some of the aspects of late Ptolemaic Alexandria. All three were directly descended from Antony, and they seem to have cultivated his memory. Their courts were notorious centres of extravagance and, notably in the cases of Gaius and Nero, of wilful cruelty. Their women dressed their hair in Alexandrian-style corkscrew locks, while the *stola*, a restricting garment introduced by Augustus, acquired a sensual allure far from the first emperor's modest intentions. After enduring decades of imperial hostility, the Egyptian sanctuaries were revived at Rome under imperial patronage, and eastern cults enjoyed considerable popularity in the more modest domestic arena, where the satirist Martial was later to joke that every artificial garden stream was named the Nile or the Euphrates. Gaius rebuilt the sanctuary of Isis begun by

Caesar, significantly located among the dynastic imperial monuments of the Campus Martius near the Tiber. In Egypt, too, the elevated status of local elites claiming descent from Greek settlers was protected by Claudius and Nero. It is tempting to see Antony's revenge from beyond the grave, or at least to speak of some long-term realisation of his dynastic ambitions and his vision of an orientalised imperial monarchy.

Cleopatra and Octavian

In the wake of the tragic drama of Cleopatra's relationship with Antony, the queen's significance to her Roman enemy Octavian is sometimes overlooked: it is here considered in further detail.

Born in Rome in 63 BC to an aristocratic family, Julius Caesar's hitherto obscure great-nephew came to public attention at the age of eighteen, when in 44 BC he was declared heir to the murdered Dictator's name and fortune. In pursuing his adoptive father's assassins, Brutus and Cassius, as in building experience and personal authority through strategic alliances, the young Octavian proved ruthless and calculating. These personal qualities were to serve him well throughout his long life.

After his defeat of Cleopatra and Mark Antony at the Battle of Actium, Octavian became master of Rome and the Mediterranean world. In 27 BC he took the name Augustus offered to him by the Roman Senate. Describing himself as the first citizen of his own restored republic, Augustus built an empire, his reforms embracing provinces, cities, armies and individual citizens. Even Roman notables were henceforth obliged to wear the Roman toga when attending formal public events in Rome. At the other end of the social spectrum, former slaves were permitted to legalise their marriages, and their children were offered citizenship. On an astonishingly broad front, Augustus defined a lasting Roman identity, establishing traditions that, though newly brought to prominence, appeared as old as Rome itself.

The emperor traced his personal descent from the exiled Trojan prince Aeneas, who provided him with an austerely heroic origin in the lands of the earliest civilisations in the eastern Mediterranean. Aeneas was emphatically an enemy of Greece, and through this invented ancestry Augustus was able to present himself as the polar opposite of the recently defeated Hellenistic Greek regimes that had supported Antony, above all Cleopatra's Egypt. Various factors, not all of them ultimately negative, determined the relationship between Cleopatra and Octavian. These specific aspects of their enmity are briefly explored here.

Caesarion

Between Cleopatra and Octavian stood the queen's first-born son, Ptolemy XV Caesarion, his nickname reflecting his likely parentage by Julius Caesar, Octavian's adoptive father. If his traditional date of birth in 47 BC is accepted, then Caesarion was nearly three years old at the time of Caesar's assassination on the Ides of March of 44 BC, and had lived most of his life in Rome. However, as we have seen, one of the pressing causes of the unpopularity that led to Caesar's murder was the widespread rumour that a way might be found to marriage between the Roman Dictator and the queen of Egypt, and the capital moved from Rome to Alexandria. In the wake of the public proclamation of Gaius Octavianus as Caesar's sole heir, Cleopatra and her entourage rapidly departed Rome for Egypt; there were rumours that she was pregnant at the time, either with Caesarion, if his birth is to be dated in the summer of 44 BC, or with a second child who did not survive. Following the convenient death of Cleopatra's then co-ruler and youngest brother Ptolemy XIV, the infant Caesarion became Ptolemy XV. The burden of rule naturally fell to Cleopatra, who nonetheless assiduously promoted her son (see p. 93).

Caesarion presented a considerable threat to Octavian: if he was Caesar's child, as was publicly recognised by Mark Antony a decade later, then he had a greater claim to Caesar's name and wealth than did Octavian. Thus, if before Caesar's death Caesarion had provided a passport to Rome for Cleopatra, in its aftermath he embodied her eventual fate. He is the only one of her children who is known to have been assassinated after the fall of Alexandria to Octavian in 30 BC, his murder signifying his importance to Rome. Cleopatra's carefully planned attempt to send him to safe exile in India beforehand equally signified his importance to Egypt.

In her systematic promotion of Caesarion as co-ruler, Cleopatra had openly courted hostility from Octavian. As both he and Antyllus, Antony's son by Fulvia, were touted as successors to their beleaguered parents, they were fatally exposed to Octavian's vengeance.

Antony

Another primary source of tension was Cleopatra's seduction in 41 BC of Octavian's fellow triumvir Mark Antony, whom Cleopatra probably knew from his role in re-establishing her father on the Egyptian throne in 54 BC. In 40 BC, the year of the birth of his twin children by Cleopatra, Antony received news that his wife Fulvia had encouraged his brother Lucius Antonius, consul at Rome in 41 BC, to revolt against Octavian. The dispute concerned land in Italy reserved for the settlement of military veterans; many considered that Octavian had taken more than his share. After a bitter siege at Perugia, Lucius Antonius was spared by Octavian, who made him governor of Spain. Fulvia was exiled to Athens, where she had to explain herself to a furious Antony. She died in Greece, and Antony moved to Italy, where after further fighting he made his peace with Octavian in the Treaty of Brundisium. The pact of peace was sealed by Antony's marriage to Octavian's sister Octavia, who was to play a major diplomatic role in mediating between the two rivals.

After the birth of the elder Antonia in the autumn of 38 BC, Antony returned to his eastern lands; he and Octavia were based at Athens, where they celebrated a sacred marriage on the Acropolis, and actively engaged with the religious, cultural and political life of the city. The following year the pact between Antony and Octavian, which had been tested by Octavian's high-handed calculations of his own needs, was renewed with Octavia's help at Tarentum in southern Italy. Having staved off by proxy the Parthian threat in the east, Antony finally decided to pursue an active campaign, and allowed the pregnant Octavia to travel only as far as Corfu. He had already calculated that, notwithstanding the evident virtues of Octavia, her brother was unreliable, and for his eastern campaigns Cleopatra would prove a firmer source of support. Thus he spent the winter of 37-6 BC with the queen of Egypt at Antioch, and celebrated their reunion with the birth of another son, Ptolemy Philadelphus. In the renewal of their liaison Cleopatra was granted important areas of land in the Levant, thereby reviving the notion of a Ptolemaic empire protecting Egypt to the north and east; she also massively increased her revenues and became an active partner in Antony's military campaigns.

In 35 BC Octavia sailed to Athens with 70 ships and 2,000 men with clothing and supplies and arms, all destined to support Antony's campaigns in Armenia and Parthia. This attempt to recall her husband to the Roman fold proved a dismal failure: he wrote to Athens requesting her to send on all her offerings but (in terms of his agreement with Octavian, reasonably) claimed that he was owed not 2,000 but 20,000 men and had no need of ships: he sent her back to Rome.

There, Antony's treatment of his wife was regarded as a public humiliation, and gave Octavian an effective pretext for raising public anger against Cleopatra without involving Caesar. Though Caesarion remained the major long-term threat, Octavian was unable to focus upon him because of the boy's relationship to his own adoptive father. Caesar's controversial role could be reconciled by virtue of his status as a god, his divinity having been proclaimed in 42 BC. After the Athens debacle, Octavia was accorded public honours by the Senate, alongside Octavian's wife Livia. Focusing upon the weaker elements in Antony's character, Octavian attacked his drunkenness and promiscuity; Antony replied with a letter listing Octavian's numerous lovers in Rome, while claiming that he himself remained faithful to Cleopatra, with whom he lived as her husband. A report of the letter has survived in an unexpected source, the Roman biographer Suetonius' life of Augustus.

Antony's gifts to Cleopatra and her family

In 34 BC the result of Antony's eastern campaigns offered further ammunition to Octavian.

First, and most outrageously in Roman eyes, Antony celebrated his triumph not in Rome but in Alexandria; as Plutarch later remarked, it seemed to the Romans as if the gifts that should have come to their gods were instead presented to the Egyptian people. The insult to Rome was compounded by the ceremony that followed the parade in the gymnasium of Alexandria, in which Antony dressed as Dionysos while Cleopatra appeared as Isis (p. 50). In a public context, these roles could be understood only as the enactment of a Greek version of the Egyptian concept of kingship: in living memory Cleopatra's father had proclaimed himself the New Dionysos and she herself had been acclaimed a goddess at the age of four. The spectacle of their six-year-old twin son Alexander dressed as an Armenian prince, crowned with a tiara and surrounded by ethnic bodyguards, followed the humiliation of the true king of Armenia, who, having been captured by Antony's troops, was paraded through Alexandria along with his family, the group trussed in golden chains. To celebrate his lordship of equally extensive lands in Syria and Asia Minor, Antony and Cleopatra's infant son Ptolemy was dressed in the distinctive Macedonian cap, the *kausia*, and was also surrounded by ethnic bodyguards. Alexander's twin sister Cleopatra Selene was granted control of Crete and Cyrenaica, thereby completing an arc of territories ceded to Cleopatra's young family for the defence of Egypt from the west, through the north and to the east. As for Caesarion, the young king of Egypt was publicly acknowledged as Caesar's son. Henceforth titled 'King of Kings', he was to remain ruler of Egypt with his mother Cleopatra.

Cleopatra's own elevated status was celebrated on silver denarii issued by Antony (Plate 9), on which she was described as *Cleopatrae Reginae regum filiorumque regum*, in English an ambiguous title which may be rendered 'For [or of] Cleopatra, Queen of kings and of the children of kings' or 'Queen of kings and of her children who are kings'. The Latin of the text jars with the eastern origin of the titles. A ship's prow depicted before the queen's portrait reminded users of the coin of the nature of her support for Antony. On the other side of the coin Antony was portrayed bareheaded with the caption *Antoni Armenia devicta*: 'For [or of] Antony, Armenia having been vanquished'. A miniature Armenian tiara in the field of Antony's portrait reminded users of the rather more northern origin of the queen's newly gained status. It must have come as a shock to Romans to see coins of standard Roman denomination portraying a foreign queen whose eastern titles were rendered in Latin and whose portrayal on the coin described a status equal to that of Antony. Such images and legends had only been used in very recent years for the Roman wives of Roman military leaders.

Antony as victim

A difficulty for Octavian lay in Antony's recent marriage to his sister Octavia, who still loved her errant husband. Moreover a number of Romans in Italy and elsewhere remained loyal to Antony, who had many admirable personal qualities. Widely perceived as a humane and popular leader of men, Antony was celebrated as an experienced and effective commander, a larger-than-life figure who enjoyed his drink and his women, drawing his exceptional physical stamina from his alleged descent from Anton, an otherwise unknown son of Hercules. By comparison Octavian was relatively untested, and appeared cold and calculating in his personal demeanour.

Octavian's solution was to present Antony as helpless victim of the Egyptian queen: Cleopatra was deprived of her own identity, never named but serving as an emblem of eastern monarchy, of decadence and depravity. At her hands, drugged with wine and sex, Antony had lost his reason. No longer fit to be the son of Anton, he had taken on the aspect of Dionysos, and had sunk into an appropriately Bacchic lifestyle which undermined his role as a commander of men. Even his sexuality was questioned, this most masculine of men derided as effeminate. Such a characterisation, focusing upon Cleopatra's undermining of Antony's Roman identity, itself linked with masculine characteristics, made the act of supporting him on Roman soil one of treachery and questioning of the supporter's manhood. Octavian also managed thereby to isolate Octavia and Caesar from any damaging involvement in the civil war that was to come. Moreover, he was also able to exaggerate the threat of Cleopatra, who became a credible enemy worthy even of defeat in civil war.

Most of what survives of Octavian's propaganda lies in the poetry written by Horace, Propertius and Virgil, and in the life of Antony composed much later by Plutarch. The tradition was long-lived and much exploited: if the first-century satirist Lucan was biting, the second-century historian Florus proved exceptionally condemning, and as late as the third century AD the Greek historian Dio Cassius was able to dismiss Antony as Cleopatra's cymbal player at Canopus. These writers have shaped western European perceptions of Cleopatra through their influence upon poets and dramatists of the Renaissance and later (p. 16ff.), although the interests of the latter group lay more in exploring the apparent contradictions in Cleopatra's character than in defining her responsibility for the fall of Antony.

Thus Cleopatra was presented as the 'fatal monster' to be chained by Caesar [Octavian], in Horace's celebrated victory song 'Nunc est bibendum …' ('Now is the time for drinking …', Horace, *Odes* 1.37). Propertius derided her as the 'harlot queen of incestuous Canopus'. Losing her name and the status so celebrated on Antony's coinage, Cleopatra became

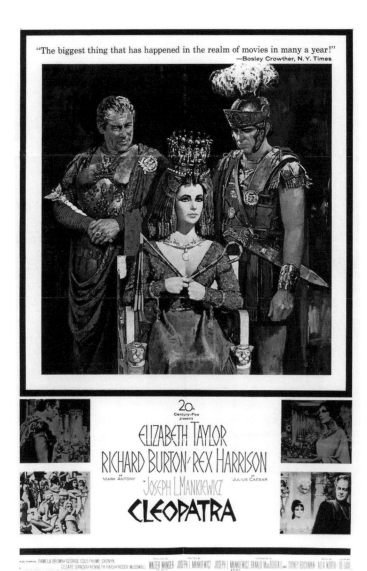

1. The defining image of Cleopatra in the mid-twentieth century: poster advertising Elizabeth Taylor as Cleopatra in Joseph L. Mankiewicz's epic film of 1963.

2. The roots of cinema in nineteenth-century European orientalism: 'Cleopatra Testing Poisons on those Condemned to Death' (oil on canvas) by Alexandre Cabanel (1823-89).

3. Cleopatra's journey from flighty princess to heroine: Renaissance Italian cameo portrait of a woman as the suicidal Cleopatra.

4. Egypt's heroine today: Cleopatra on a contemporary packet of cigarettes.

5. Defining the authentic Egyptian Cleopatra: detail of an ancient statuette of Cleopatra with a cartouche of disputed antiquity giving her name.

6. The orientalist vision: Cleopatra seduces Caesar. 'Cleopatra' by A. Benini (1879) (oil on canvas).

7. Ancient orientalism: Antony (*left*) and Cleopatra (*right*) in oriental guise on silver tetradrachms minted for Antony's eastern campaigns.

8. Silver tetradrachm of Cleopatra's great-aunt, Cleopatra Thea, perhaps the model for Cleopatra's eastern coin portraits.

9. Ancient multi-culturalism: silver *denarius* of Antony, Roman tribune, and Cleopatra, Queen of Kings and of her children who are (the children of?) kings.

10. The Greek goddess: bronze coin minted on Cyprus, showing (a, *left*) Cleopatra nursing the infant Caesarion, and (b, *right*) on the reverse, the double cornucopia used as a symbol of Egypt's prosperity by Cleopatra and her distant predecessor Arsinoe II.

11. The conventional Greek queen: bronze eighty-drachma coin of Cleopatra minted in Alexandria.

12. The protégée of Caesar: silver coin with a portrait of Cleopatra minted in Askalon.

13. A Roman perspective: Side A of the Portland Vase, a wine-jar perhaps recalling the fatal seduction of Antony by Cleopatra. Blown glass carved in the cameo technique a decade or so after the fall of Alexandria in 30 BC.

14. Roman caricature: a woman resembling Cleopatra profanes a ceremony honouring the death and resurrection of Osiris. Roman terracotta lamp made in Italy, about AD 50-80.

15. The defender of Egypt: portrait of Cleopatra from her daughter Cleopatra Selene's capital city of Iol Caesarea, Mauretania (modern Cherchel, Algeria).

16. Identifying Cleopatra as Egyptian queen: head from a limestone statuette of Cleopatra wearing the triple *uraeus*.

17. Cleopatra remembered in Rome: marble portrait head of Cleopatra from the site of the Villa of the Quintilii, near Rome.

18. Sources for Cleopatra's status in Egypt: the Kushite 'god's wife' Shepenwepet makes offerings to her predecessor Amenirdas in the latter's tomb at Medinat Habu.

19. Royal mother: Cleopatra and Caesarion make offerings to the gods on the south wall of the Temple of Hathor at Dendera.

20. Cleopatra's inspiration: inscribed statuette of Arsinoe II.

21. Cleopatra as queen of Egypt: black basalt statue with triple uraeus and double cornucopia.

22. (a, *above*) Divine mother and (b, *below*) royal son: from a colossal statue group of Cleopatra as Isis and Ptolemy XV Caesarion.

23. The young Cleopatra? Fragment of a basalt statue of a youthful queen.

24. Cleopatra defaced? Colossal statue from Canopus perhaps representing Cleopatra as a deified queen, the face deliberately removed.

the embodiment of the threat to Roman virility from Egyptian voluptuousness. In this invective, even the use of mosquito nets by Cleopatra's troops was regarded as unmanly, and the threat that those nets might be spread on the Tarpeian rock by the Roman Capitolium was inconceivable. Cleopatra, like Antony, was said to drink intemperately, and to wear a ring celebrating this fact. Some slurs were perhaps unintentionally comic: Pliny's account of Cleopatra tearing from her ear a priceless pearl earring, to dissolve it in a cup of vinegar and then drink it, much to the dismay of Antony and Plancus, proved an irresistible image to Renaissance and later European artists.

It has recently been suggested that some of the stone and glass cameos and intaglios that were so distinguished a feature of art of the early empire were intended as illustrations of the poetry, that is, as objects commissioned individually, apparently for contemplation of the human causes of war alongside celebration of Octavian's hard-worn victory.

Thus the Portland Vase, now in the collections of the British Museum but originating from Rome, may represent on one side the seduction by Cleopatra of Antony, the latter shown in Dionysiac guise, to the dismay of Antony, and on the other the consequent abandonment of Octavia, who is comforted by Octavian, while he in his turn is reassured of eventual victory by his divine patron Venus Genetrix (Plate 13). On this reading the historical context would follow Antony's rejection of Octavia in 35 BC.

Similarly the Carpegna cameo, now in the Louvre but also originating from a collection in Renaissance Rome, may show Antony's intoxication at the hands of Cleopatra.

Dressed as a corpulent unwreathed Dionysos, he reclines in drunken stupor in the lap of a woman bearing Cleopatra's hairstyle, eastern royal dress and facial features. A satyr to the left recoils from the scene, finding it hard to believe that the pair need another round of drinks from the horn he carries on his head. The central figures find counterparts in two wall-paintings of Pompeii, of which the better preserved example in the Villa of the Mysteries may represent the drunken Dionysos reclining in the lap of his mother Semele. However, in the cameo the couple appear to recline on a pile of masonry, possibly representing the tower of a city wall. To the right, a smirking panther accompanies an exultant satyr with African features: could the masonry and the satyr suggest that the scene is set in Alexandria?

The visual language of cameo glass, traditionally thought to be an Alexandrian craft transposed to Rome in the wake of Actium, offers on this reading a harsh commentary from a Roman viewpoint on the excesses of life as enjoyed in Antony and Cleopatra's Alexandria. Similarly unfavourable commentaries appear in wall-paintings and mosaics of the later first and second-century AD, and caricatures of Cleopatra may also appear on Roman lamps, many of which were used by the army in forts on or near the Rhine/Danube frontier (Plate 14). It is not clear whether the naked woman with Cleopatra's hair and features depicted on the discus of the lamp served as a pin-up or a warning. Recently it has been suggested that the scene in which the woman sits on a dismembered phallus, mounted on a crocodile within a Nilotic landscape, represents a sexual violation of the lost phallus of Osiris, in traditional Egyptian religion the object of veneration. In Roman paintings, mosaics and terracotta and stone reliefs, the Nilotic landscape, setting of ancient Egyptian religious rites carefully observed for the benefit of her subjects by Cleopatra, was similarly profaned by its use for caricatured scenes of excessive sex and drinking.

Against the current of anti-Egyptian propaganda, a pro-Alexandrian reaction is clear within the reigns of the later Julio-Claudian emperors Caligula, Claudius and Nero (p. 55). However, Nero's eventual successor Vespasian (AD 69-79) embodied a return to the traditional values of Roman Italy, and it is possible that many surviving caricatures were commissioned in his reign, notably those of the latest phase of occupation at Pompeii, destroyed in AD 79. The tension between traditional Roman and Hellenistic Greek ideas of culture and lifestyle was not resolved until the era of the emperor Hadrian (AD 117-138), who eagerly embraced Greek culture while energetically promoting a vision of one undivided empire with a fixed frontier. It was in the more relaxed cultural ambience of the early second century AD that Plutarch composed his life of Antony.

Octavian as a foil to Cleopatra's integrity

If the propaganda unleashed by Octavian did long-term damage to Cleopatra's image in Rome and even Renaissance and modern Europe, one aspect of their relationship, albeit tragic, showed Cleopatra in a favourable light. This concerns her negotiations with Octavian in the wake of the fall of Alexandria, and her subsequent suicide, following that of Antony, who had died in her arms.

When, after routing Antony and Cleopatra at Actium, Octavian arrived in Phoenicia, he received Cleopatra's royal insignia: she was ready to abdicate, but asked that Octavian permit the Egyptian throne to pass to her children. Octavian accepted the insignia, but gave an unclear reply, also to a second envoy, their children's tutor Euphronius, who arrived with a large bribe. Determined to place her personal treasure beyond Octavian's reach, Cleopatra walled it within 'high monuments and tombs of great beauty near the Temple of Isis in Alexandria', as Plutarch has it. Equally concerned to acquire the treasure, and worried that Cleopatra might burn it in desperation, Octavian offered good terms as he took the frontier post of Paraetonium and the eastern Nile city of Pelusium. But after Antony's attempts to repulse Octavian's troops had failed, and it became clear that he and Cleopatra lacked sufficient support for their cause, suicide became an option.

The greatest effect of Cleopatra's death was her ennoblement. She suddenly seemed, and was to remain, a much more substantial figure than Octavian. She had denied him and killed herself for love of Antony. In this act, against all expectations, Cleopatra had shown herself capable of great personal integrity. This unexpected virtue was celebrated by Horace in the very same ode (1.37) in which, as we have seen, the 'fatal monster' was derided:

Yet she, seeking to perish in nobler fashion, displayed no womanly fear for the dagger's point, nor did she seek out secret shores with her speedy fleet.

Daring to gaze with serene countenance upon her fallen

palace, bravely handling poisonous snakes to draw their dark venom to her body, ever bolder as she determined to die; scorning, it seems, the fate of being dragged off as a private citizen in hostile galleys to grace a glorious triumph – she was no humble woman!

Cleopatra's Royal Image in the Greek and Roman World

We possess no authentic portrait of Cleopatra, and the features of the Queen have left not the slightest reflection on this vast earth where she caused so much mourning and misfortune ....

This was the judgement of Anatole France in his preface to an edition of Théophile Gautier's *Cléopâtre*, first published in 1845. Such a negative reaction reflects the mosaic of surviving scraps of evidence, which offer no consistent portrait but tell us more about those who created these very disparate images of Cleopatra – her Roman detractors; her fearful, even grateful subjects; and perhaps even the queen herself. Other modern writers have used the gaps in our knowledge to promote an air of mystery: 'It is as if the darkness closes around her', wrote Enzo Gualazzi in 1992.

What, then, has survived? At least in the course of Cleopatra's twenty-one-year reign the Alexandrian authorities issued various denominations of coins bearing her portrait (Plate 11). The queen's image also appears on a coin of Cyprus, apparently celebrating the birth of Caesarion (Plate 10), and on coins issued in various cities in Cilicia and Syria-Palestina following the campaigns of Antony in Armenia and

Parthia and the granting of lands in the east to Cleopatra and her children (Plate 7). These coins were handled by large numbers of people, some of the issues remaining in circulation for years after Cleopatra's death and reaching lands as far from Egypt as Britain.

All the surviving coins offer images of Cleopatra in the naturalistic style developed in the kingdoms of the successors to Alexander the Great, but they vary considerably in their presentation. The image on the Cyprus coin, for example, evidently portrays Cleopatra as a goddess, while the eastern issues (often mistakenly interpreted as examples of Roman hyper-realism) show her as a senior monarch in the Mesopotamian tradition. Meanwhile the Alexandrian issues, which constitute the largest surviving group of portraits, show Cleopatra as an unexceptional ruler in the Ptolemaic tradition. These significant variations reflect Cleopatra's personal range as a ruler, her close connection to Antony, their sensitivity to local notions of kingship, and the likelihood that some local issues escaped their control: a number of the portraits are distinctly unflattering.

Some marble portrait heads of Cleopatra have also survived, and these may be compared to the coinage: one (Plate 15), from Cherchel in Mauretania (Algeria) is close to the Mesopotamian types – if indeed it does represent Cleopatra and not her daughter Cleopatra Selene, who eventually came to rule Mauretania as consort to Juba II, client-king of Rome. Very recently it has been proposed that Cleopatra may be recognised on Roman cameo glass and in wall-paintings (pp. 65-6 and Plate 13). These images, too, are based on the Alexandrian coin portraits, though coloured by

Roman hatred of the Egyptian queen and the need to deliver a specific narrative, in which Cleopatra might be likened to the Egyptian goddess Isis.

Cleopatra on Alexandrian coinage

Cleopatra's Alexandrian coinage is difficult to date precisely within her reign. There is, then, little sense of the ageing of Cleopatra from a seventeen-year-old princess on her accession in 51 BC to the mature mother of four and survivor of a tumultuous reign at the time of her death by suicide twenty-one years later. Throughout, Cleopatra's hair was dressed in the 'melon coiffure', so called after its resemblance to the segments of a cantaloupe melon. To achieve the effect, the hair is drawn back from the brow in a series of tight braids woven into a large bun at the nape of the neck. A broad and flattish diadem is tied beneath or threaded through the bun. The face is surrounded by distinctive 'kiss-curls'. These also appear beneath the wig on some of Cleopatra's Egyptian-style images (Plate 16). If dress is shown on the coinage, it takes the form of a simple mantle swathed around the shoulders. The queen sometimes wears jewellery – a single strand of pearls around the neck, and drop earrings, only one of which is visible in profile images.

Cleopatra had distinctive features, most notably a strongly hooked aquiline nose, the subject of much jesting and speculation by European commentators, among them the French mathematician and philosopher Blaise Pascal, who in 1670 penned his famous aphorism 'Had Cleopatra's nose been shorter, the face of the world would have changed.' The queen's nose was even the subject of a wartime novel by the eccentric British celebrity Gerald Tyrwhitt, Lord Berners, who published *The Romance of the Nose* in 1941. Indeed, at the time of writing in summer 2005, a play on the same subject was broadcast on BBC Radio 3.

The offending feature does not seem to have occasioned so much surprise among her contemporaries, who may have seen the queen's nose as a sign of beauty and eastern-style authority. However, in some portraits the queen's features were exaggerated, and in others they were subsumed within an idealised image of the monarch. It is not always easy to identify the reasons for such presentations. For example, a coin minted in the free city of Askalon in 48/9 BC (Plate 12) may (from its date) celebrate Caesar's restoration of Cleopatra to the Egyptian throne, though the act is not commemorated in any legend on the coin: the portrait shows the young queen with an unexpectedly scrawny neck, in an apparent nod to the realistic style of Caesar's own portraits, then still to appear on his coinage. In contrast, another issue made in Askalon just over a decade later offers a more idealised presentation of Cleopatra, perhaps celebrating Antony's return to her after his brief marriage to Octavia. The two images of Cleopatra circulated together alongside the city's more customary image of the long-dead Antiochus VIII Grypos, the Syrian king who had granted Askalon its independence in 104 BC, from which era the coins were dated even in Cleopatra's day.

Marble portraits in Alexandrian Greek style

Despite the many variations, the Alexandrian coins achieved a wide circulation for the length of Cleopatra's reign, and evidently provided the model for images of the queen in some other media in the Roman west. Thus the marble portrait head of Cleopatra from the Villa of the Quintilii near Rome (Plate 17), now in the Vatican Museums, was eventually identified from its close resemblance to the portraits on Alexandrian coinage. Nonetheless this head has the unusual and still misunderstood feature of a knot of hair standing proud of the head in front of the diadem. This has often been taken as a concession to the Roman viewer of the sculpture, which was most likely commissioned some years after Cleopatra's death. On this reading the knot of hair represents the Roman *nodus*, a roll of hair above the brow much favoured by noble Roman ladies of Cleopatra's day. However, the conventional Roman *nodus* is much broader, and the hair is normally taken back from it in an elaborate plait across the crown of the head to the bun at the nape of the neck. In contrast, Cleopatra's knot is compact and isolated. Moreover on her left cheek is a raised stone scar, evidently not a mason's measuring mark, but the remains of an attribute or another figure. The head was found with a draped torso of a type associated with the corn goddess Ceres (Greek Demeter). It is worth considering whether Cleopatra was here represented as a goddess, the knot of hair a sign of her divine authority.

Other stone heads include a more idealised head of Parian marble now in Berlin, found like the Vatican head in the Roman Campagna at about the same time, towards the end of the eighteenth century. The antiquity of this head has been questioned, but the evidence of its surface and collection history suggests that such doubts are misplaced.

Eastern influence upon later portraits of Cleopatra

Another marble head, the only known example of its kind from Egypt itself, is now in Paris, in the Louvre Museum. In this small work the sculptor has emphasised the curls around the face, an especially prominent feature of Cleopatra's later portraits. Indeed, in the later years of Cleopatra's reign the hairstyle changes in other respects, the hair in front of the diadem becoming much less constrained, while the bun at the nape shrinks in size, the overall effect being the deconstruction of the tightly constrained 'melon coiffure'. The diadem too is narrower. A similar vision is presented in the large Parian marble head found in Cherchel (Plate 15).

These features also appear on the eastern coinage, where Cleopatra was often portrayed with her companion and patron Mark Antony, each ruler occupying one face of the coin (p. 49, Plate 7). The city of Dora in Syria-Palestina issued images of them side by side, suggesting they were married, but no written evidence survives of any such contract. This type of portrait is also found on silver denarii apparently issued by Cleopatra at an unknown eastern mint (p. 62, Plate 9). The legend on the coin refers to the titles and lands awarded to Cleopatra and her children by Antony in 34 BC (p. 50, Fig. 5). Antony himself appears on the reverse of the coin, his image, like Cleopatra's, massive and block-like, ending at the neck, with no drapery. The concept of 'Queen of Kings' is an eastern one. Although Cleopatra has the exaggerated features typical of eastern rulers, she wears a heavy necklace across her throat with a mantle caught at the shoulder in western style, the tie of her diadem elaborately looped through the catch. On other coins in which she appears with Antony (Plate 7), the dress matches more closely the eastern title: the queen wears a ceremonial mantle, the edges decorated with beads (probably pearls), which serve to emphasise the breasts. On these coins Cleopatra wears a bead necklace around her throat, looped through a large button on her shoulder, from which falls a metal bar. The diadem here has a ladder-like fringe. The mantle and necklace recall the dress of Mesopotamian queens of the first century BC.

Unexpectedly, this type of portrait antedates the settlement in 34 BC of titles and lands known as the 'Donations of Alexandria' (p. 50, Fig. 5). It may have to do with Antony's return to Cleopatra in 37 BC and her support for his eastern campaigns. The new portrait style appears in the city of Damascus in Syria, never under Cleopatra's direct authority, in 37/6 BC. Here a reference may have been intended to Cleopatra's formidable great-aunt Cleopatra Thea (p. 35, Plate 8).

Images of Cleopatra as a goddess

Some scholars have translated Thea as 'goddess', and indeed Cleopatra had been proclaimed a goddess at the age of four. But in the coins described above no visual signs of godlike status appear, and the proposal that the coins show Cleopatra as the eventual successor to her great-aunt Cleopatra Thea carries more conviction. Conversely, the bronze coin minted in Cyprus (Plate 10a) shows Cleopatra in Greek style, but wearing the *stephane* or raised diadem indicative of divinity. The queen, named in the Greek legend as 'Queen Cleopatra', carries a sceptre over her shoulder as a symbol of divine authority. In front of her a somewhat shapeless blob represents the infant Caesarion. This evidently divine image was intended for western consumption. It also appears on the royal seals from Edfu, Egypt. If the statue of Cleopatra in Caesar's Temple of Venus the Mother in his Forum in Rome had survived, it would possibly have looked rather like a colossal version of these miniature images, and have used these signs of divine status.

Identifying Cleopatra's portraits

Though the Vatican head and most likely the Berlin portrait were known from the late eighteenth century, the Vatican head was identified as Cleopatra only in 1933. Until then the surviving images of the queen were not subjected to the rigorous analysis of comparing sculptured heads to named coin portraits, long used to identify sculptured images of Roman emperors and empresses. The association of the Vatican head with the torso of the goddess Ceres may have proved a deterrent, and many misidentifications stood in the way of unbiased scholarship. However, for post-Renaissance Europe, the greater obstacle to understanding Cleopatra's images proved the drama of the queen's life and death, especially her tragic romance with Antony. This overwhelmed all other considerations and apparently inhibited western scholars from examining the queen as a working monarch.

Indeed, Cleopatra's suicide for love of Antony continues to dominate perceptions of the queen in western Europe, and the very disparate nature of the surviving ancient representations of Cleopatra has not helped us to form a coherent account of her portraiture. There is little evidence to suggest tight central control in antiquity over the form of Cleopatra's image, and plenty to support the view that many portraits were locally inspired or directed by Cleopatra and her advisers at a particular local audience. It has also proved difficult to identify negative images of the queen in Roman art, because the Romans were interested in exploring the fall of Antony at the hands of the queen, and consequently focused upon his fate and, more generally, the moral laxity of Cleopatra's Egypt. The result of this was a deliberate loss of focus on the representation of the queen as an individual ruler. This stands in marked contrast to post-Renaissance dramatists and artists, who were fascinated by Cleopatra's moral journey from extravagant princess to tragic queen and not much interested in Antony.

The surviving Roman images, then, created after Cleopatra's death, concentrated upon the queen's alleged drunkenness and seductive power. She is dishevelled if not naked, and has lost the signs of her identity as queen, becoming the 'fatal monster' of Horace's ode (p. 64). Her suicide proved at best an ambivalent development from the Roman point of view: it disposed of a potentially awkward dilemma for the Roman authorities, but Cleopatra's death cheated Octavian of the chance to parade the defeated queen in his triumph at Rome. He had to make do with her surviving children and a portable image of the dying queen, which (contrary to some modern scholarly opinion) has not survived. Such images really did make myth of the reality of Cleopatra's long and challenging reign.

4

Cleopatra as Queen of Egypt

Throughout history Egypt has proved as alluring and intriguing as Cleopatra herself. It seems incongruous, then, that the queen's presentation in her homeland is often neglected by modern biographers. Part of the problem lies in deciphering the evidence. As modern investigators we must attempt to interpret the material that has survived, in the knowledge that not even the Egyptian statues of the last Ptolemaic queen were unaffected by the Roman conquest of Egypt and the subsequent use of these objects.

Most modern studies of Cleopatra have concentrated on her international image, that is to say the presentation of the queen to Greeks and Romans abroad, most notably on the coinage minted both in Alexandria and in overseas Ptolemaic possessions (see Chapter 3). This form of image was highly political: it was vitally important that whoever saw the royal portrait recognised the ruler and the encoded messages of authenticity and continuity. Egyptian-style representations work very much in the same way. They were developed in consultation with the Egyptian priesthood, who controlled the temples and also determined the form of religious statuary.

The process of assigning a specific image to a ruler is recorded in both the Canopus and Rosetta decrees, respectively in 238 BC for the princess Berenike, daughter of

Ptolemy III and Berenike II, and in 196 BC for Ptolemy V. The knowledge derived from reading these famous multi-lingual texts helps us estimate the degree of continuity that can be expected from a series of visual images of Ptolemaic queens covering a period of three hundred years, from the time of Arsinoe II, wife of Ptolemy II, until the reign of Cleopatra VII.

Like their Pharaonic predecessors, Ptolemaic officials and artists needed to strike a careful balance between associating a queen with a predecessor or consort, but at the same time distinguishing her as the principal wife of the king. From the New Kingdom this had been achieved by using a series of specific titles, and, on a more basic iconographic level, by introducing more than one royal cobra on the brow of the principal royal woman. The leading royal female could be the mother of the king, or his principal wife; she was often also the mother of the future ruler, and the number of royal cobras reflected her status in these various roles. This partic-ular practice was copied by some Ptolemaic queens. The uraeus (or cobra) also offered protection by reference to the sun god Ra, and was generally understood as a marker of royalty or divinity. Some Egyptian royal women were also shown wearing a headdress in the form of a vulture's head and feathers; this marked them as divine beings.

Egyptian role models

There was an obvious association of the principal wife of a king with the goddess Isis, who in the Egyptian religious pantheon was the mother of Horus and the wife of her brother Osiris. These two male gods were respectively associated with the living and deceased king of Egypt, making Isis an essential role model for powerful royal women. Cleopatra III was the first Ptolemaic queen to assimilate herself directly with the goddess, and she was followed by Cleopatra VII, who called herself the New Isis.

There was also no shortage of royal role models for Cleopatra's Egyptian imagery. Earlier Ptolemaic queens such as Arsinoe II and powerful Egyptian royal women of the Pharaonic period had been separated out and given a specific iconography in order to distinguish them from others in the royal court. Thus Tiye, the wife of Amenhotep III and mother of Akhenaten; Nefertiti, the principal wife of Akhenaten; Nefertari, the wife, and Merytamun the daughter and wife of Ramesses II were each given a specific attribute to distinguish them. Interestingly, the female consorts of the Kushite rulers from ancient Sudan, who formed the twenty-fifth dynasty, were also awarded a specific attribute in their images. These queens wore the divine vulture headdress and the double uraeus. They were also given the divine role of the 'god's wife of Amun' and as such appeared as the god's consorts. This office offered material wealth as well as divine status and often brought a political role in the choice of successors.

At the tomb of the Kushite queen Amenirdas at Medinat Habu on the West Bank at Thebes, her successor Shepenwepet makes offerings to the deceased 'god's wife' (Plate 18). The former wears the vulture cap, stressing her divinity, and the latter the more generic cobra on her brow. The chapels and chambers of the tomb served two purposes:

to promote the divine status of the deceased queen, and to stress the links between Amenirdas and her successor Shepenwepet. The result is an intimate exchange of offerings between the two women. This building and the meaningful scenes portrayed on its walls may well have served as a direct model for the cult of the deceased Ptolemaic queen Arsinoe II. However, the bond between the Ptolemaic queens was not as strong as that of their Kushite predecessors, and in the case of Arsinoe II it is her brother/consort who offers to her on the temple reliefs at Philae. Two hundred and fifty years later Cleopatra VII would stress her paternal links by taking the title Philopator (father-loving) rather than showing her allegiance to a female member of the dynasty. There may, however, be other means by which the last Ptolemaic queen linked herself to one of the dynasty's earliest.

Unlike the Kushite royal women, the early Ptolemaic queens were not initially perceived as automatically divine during their lifetimes. There were three steps to becoming a living god. First and most commonly in the third century BC, rulers and their queens would associate themselves with the name of an established deity. This was common in Egyptian culture, and indeed their Egyptian subjects would have had no problem in seeing their Macedonian Greek rulers as divine beings; quite the contrary. In contrast, the idea of living divine rulers was new to the Greeks. Alexander of Macedon had played with the notion of divinity by associating himself with Zeus Ammon, but Alexander also enjoyed a heroic status which none of his successors had earned. For the Ptolemies an alternative style was required, and the dynastic cult was the principal means of introducing the notion of deification of the living rulers, by which pairs of rulers adopted divine status. This ideology clearly had its roots in Egyptian kingship, and was perhaps more acceptable to the Greeks because it was the office itself that was divine, a status accorded to its holders only by right of association.

It is, then, almost as if the Egyptian priests turned to a history book when asked by Ptolemy II to distinguish the images of his sister and second wife, Arsinoe II, from those of his first wife, Arsinoe I. Arsinoe II adopted two cobras as others had before her: to distinguish her from her predecessor, but also to represent her supreme power as the principal royal female. It has also been suggested that the double uraeus might represent the two sibling rulers, although there is no earlier precedent for this interpretation.

The second step to deification was an honour awarded after death, to elevate the status of a royal individual. Deceased Ptolemaic queens might thus appear as goddesses, receiving rather than offering to the gods. Arsinoe II is notable in that she appears soon after her death in the decoration of the walls of the Temple of Isis at Philae, where she stands behind the goddess and receives an offering from her consort Ptolemy II. Later, on the south gateway at Karnak temple, Arsinoe appears with her brother/husband receiving offerings from their 'son' Ptolemy III, who was in fact the result of his father's first marriage. Other third-century BC queens were worshipped after their deaths as part of the dynastic cult, but only Arsinoe II appeared with established deities as just described.

A difficulty in establishing the identity of individual queens in the art of the Ptolemaic period is that the facial features that appear on the earliest sculptures seem to have been reproduced until the first century BC. It is therefore difficult to date purely Egyptian-style female royal sculptures unless there is a distinguishing feature such as an inscription, a personal attribute or an Egyptian-style portrait feature that emulates those of the male rulers on their Greek-style representations. As noted, we know from inscribed statues and cult vases that Arsinoe II was portrayed with a double uraeus and a double cornucopia (horn of plenty) both during her lifetime and after her death. The latter symbol was Greek in origin and appears in its double form on coins, vases and statues in both the Greek and Egyptian traditions.

A similar scenario can be imagined in 44 BC when Cleopatra VII announced the period of her 'new rule' with her son Caesarion as her consort. The queen needed a visual feature that would commemorate and announce the new reign. It is also possible that Cleopatra VII needed to associate herself with an earlier queen in order to stress her right to rule Egypt. Many of her predecessors had adopted a dominant role. For instance, Berenike II appeared with her husband on the walls of the Temple of Opet at Karnak in a ceremonial dress worn by male rulers, while Cleopatra III can be seen on the temples of Khonsu at Karnak and the birth-temple (*mammisi*) at Deir el-Medina, with her son Ptolemy IX standing behind her in a subservient pose. Cleopatra VII would later mimic this order on the shrine of Geb at Koptos, taking the dominant role in the offering scene.

From the time of Cleopatra I (194-176 BC), we find royal women as living goddesses in their own right, and the early Cleopatras left no doubt over their divine status. Cleopatra I appeared as a goddess during her lifetime and foreshadowed the role of Cleopatra VII in ruling Egypt as regent to her son. Cleopatra III (141-101 BC) was in many respects the first to promote her own deification and her role as priest of a variety of cults that had previously been associated with the male ruler. Like Cleopatra VII, the third Cleopatra ruled with her sons. Such was her power that some scholars have suggested that she too may have worn a multiple uraeus.

It is during the reign of Cleopatra III (141-101 BC) that we find the third form of deification. This Ptolemaic queen believed herself to be the living embodiment of the Egyptian deity Isis. The concept was taken a step further by Cleopatra VII's father and by the queen herself. Rather than simply embodying existing gods, Cleopatra VII and her father became 'new' versions of Isis and Dionysos, calling themselves 'Nea Isis' and 'Neos Dionysos'.

Distinguishing Egyptian-style representations of Ptolemaic queens

Decrees such as those surviving on the stones from Rosetta and Canopus suggest that the priests established a form for an individual's divine royal statue and that this imagery was then copied in temples throughout Egypt. However, surviving temple reliefs are less consistent than these texts suggest, and Cleopatra II or III, even Cleopatra VII, can be found wearing the crown of Arsinoe II on certain occasions. For example, an unnamed queen is portrayed on the reliefs decorating the walls of a corridor of the Temple of Hathor at Denderah. She appears on most registers with the usual crown consisting of two plumes, a sun-disk and cow's horns, but in one scene she wears Arsinoe's crown. Given the unequivocal identification of the inscribed reliefs on the south wall of the temple (Plate 19), it is likely that the queen is to be identified as Cleopatra VII, accompanied by her son Ptolemy XV Caesarion.

If the decrees are to be taken literally there was clearly a distinction between statues carved in the round and figures carved in relief. For we find Ptolemy V, the subject of the Rosetta Stone, described as having a very specific type of statue, but appearing on temple reliefs with a variety of crowns depending on his role during any one offering scene. On the walls of temples Arsinoe II wears a vulture headdress with her specific crown but never the double uraeus so prominent in free-standing images of this queen (Plate 20).

Most Egyptian-style statues of Ptolemaic queens show them with a single cobra on their brow, and on certain statues the queens hold a single horn of plenty, or cornucopia. However, a small group of images shows queens with two or three cobras on their brow and with a double form of cornucopia. Analysis of style goes some way to establishing consistency at a given date: all the statues with three cobras appear to be of the same period. The formality of the conventions establishing royal iconography for individual rulers suggests that it is unlikely that Arsinoe II would have switched from a double to triple uraeus. The latter was, after all, a Ptolemaic development and is significantly not found on statues with early features. However, there is no single interpretation of the multiple cobras that can suit all their artistic contexts.

The striking continuity in Arsinoe II's images reflects the situation after her untimely death, when there was no political reason to change her affiliations or cult titles as was the case for queens enjoying longer and more complex reigns. In contrast, Cleopatra II ruled with two brothers, and Cleopatra III with her uncle and mother and then her two sons; finally Cleopatra VII ruled with her father, two successive brothers and then her eldest son.

The problem of identifying individual rulers is exacerbated by the lack of inscribed statues. It is clear from the inscribed evidence that Arsinoe II, as mentioned above, can be associated with the double uraeus and double cornucopia and that Cleopatra VII also used the double horn on her coins that were minted in Cyprus to celebrate the birth of Caesarion, probably in 44 BC (Plate 10b), an event which may well have been a turning point in the queen's presentation. It has been suggested, though scholars do not agree on the identification of the statues in question, that Cleopatra VII consistently wore a triple uraeus.

Statues of Cleopatra VII from Egypt

No Greek-style sculptures of Cleopatra can be securely linked with Egypt. A small-scale head now in Paris, in the Louvre Museum, is thought to have come from Egypt but is without a certain provenance. There were doubtless Greek-style representations of the queen that were known to artists in her home country, not least the queen's portrait on coinage minted in Alexandria, though it is fair to say that these representations served an international rather than a domestic audience. However, a closer look at some of the recently identified images of the queen indicates a strong link between her

Greek and Egyptian statues, suggesting that artists were aware of a central model.

There are two images in Egyptian style that can be linked to the Greek portraits of Cleopatra VII: an almost complete statue in the Metropolitan Museum of Art, New York (detail, Plate 5) and a second more fragmentary statue now in the Brooklyn Museum of Art (Plate 16). They share specific features and would when complete have been very similar in form. Both images have in common the form of the supporting back pillar, the presence of the triple uraeus, and a corkscrew wig over a fringe of natural hair, the latter in the form of snail-shell curls. It is this last feature, representing the hair of the subject beneath the wig, that directly links the two statues with Cleopatra VII. On her Greek and Roman portraits, the queen wears her hair in a bun and so-called melon coiffure, but the fringe is typically indicated by small snail-shell curls, very similar to the more stylised versions of the two New York statues (Plate 16). The wig, part of the Ptolemaic Greek repertoire perhaps adopted by Egyptian artists when representing Ptolemaic royal women as goddesses, is longer than earlier examples, falling onto the shoulders. The portrait features on the two statues are slightly different. The Brooklyn statue has fuller lips and a more youthful appearance; this statue is very similar to a fragment now in Turin (see below) and recalls the softer features that appear on a statue of Cleopatra as an Egyptian goddess found in Rome (see also below).

The Metropolitan Museum's statue (detail, Plate 5) is less carefully rendered and the artist has chosen to show a more generic portrait type with a trace of the archaic smile, a feature of Ptolemaic Egyptian sculpture from the fourth to the first centuries BC. The lips are narrow and, like the other facial features, finely chiselled. That both statues are similar in terms of their features if not style suggests that they were carved at the same time but by different artists or workshops, both interpreting the same model. Unexpectedly the Metropolitan's statue holds a single cornucopia. The lack of a double cornucopia is acceptable for Cleopatra VII because the queen did not consistently use the double form on her coinage; however, it does mean that the statue is unlikely to represent Arsinoe II, who always used the motif in double form.

The Metropolitan Museum of Art's statue has one other feature of further interest: a cartouche spelling 'Cleopatra' on the upper right arm (Plate 5). Many scholars have questioned the authenticity of this inscription, although all are agreed that the statue itself is ancient. The placement on the upper arm is certainly unusual for this period and, if the inscription is genuine, this would be the only first-century BC statue to be inscribed with a name.

Both of the statues now in New York have a triple uraeus, a motif that some scholars believe can be associated with Cleopatra VII. A third Egyptian-style statue, now in the Hermitage Museum, St Petersburg (Plate 21) shows a female figure wearing three cobras on her brow and holding a double cornucopia. This statue must represent one of only two Egyptian queens: Arsinoe II or Cleopatra VII. The image takes Egyptian form: the subject wears a sheath-like dress, an Egyptian tripartite wig and strides forwards onto the left leg, supported by a back pillar in the traditional Egyptian style. Unfortunately the pillar is uninscribed. The presentation of the subject's personal features, notably the downturned mouth combined with a strong, prominent chin, compare well with statues known to date from the late Ptolemaic period. Moreover, these particular features are shared by a group of statues representing a youthful male, who is typically identified as Caesarion or one of his brothers.

There are two other forms of statue linked with the presentation of Cleopatra VII in Egypt. One shows her as divine, the other as a ruler. We know that Cleopatra was regarded as divine during her lifetime from an inscribed stone dating to her early reign, which describes her as *thea* (goddess). The image that decorated the top of this block shows an Egyptian-style male pharaoh making an offering to Isis and Harpocrates. However, a closer inspection of the piece shows that it was re-used and so re-dedicated on behalf of the queen.

Unlike Hatshepsut, the Eighteenth Dynasty female ruler of Egypt, Cleopatra VII did not often adopt male costume. There is, however, an early Ptolemaic precedent for royal cross-dressing. As previously mentioned, on the reliefs of the Temple of Opet at Karnak, Berenike II is shown wearing a ceremonial costume more usually associated with male rulers. Cleopatra, in contrast, chose to exploit her feminine qualities. It is of little surprise, then, that the queen should choose to associate herself directly with the goddess Isis, both in her title as the New Isis and also on one of her statues.

The fragment in question is part of a two-figured representation, or dyad (Plate 22). The queen's consort (Plate 22b) is youthful in appearance and is likely to be her son and co-ruler Caesarion on account of the *hm.hmt* crown (associated with the young Horus) and a sceptre, just visible on his left shoulder. Cleopatra is completely assimilated to Isis while the male figure retains a human aspect, if not individually recognisable. In this colossal image, Cleopatra VII wears the vulture headdress (Plate 22a). The statue is idealised and archaic in style, recalling the art of the early Ptolemaic period. Were it not for the male figure accompanying the figure of Isis, the latter could easily be placed in the third century BC. The statues form a joined pair and are discussed fully below in the context of the sanctuary in which they were found (p. 104). The female figure wears a simple vulture headdress and no uraeus, stressing her divine rather than her royal status. The statue thus represents the complete apotheosis of Cleopatra and her assimilation to Isis – she has become the goddess and is presented as such.

Another surviving image of Cleopatra as goddess is the fragment of a seated statue in the Egyptian Museum, Turin. The subject wears a sheath-like dress with the traditional tripartite wig, but in place of the usual diadem or cobras set directly on the brow of the wig, this statue has a vulture headdress – the mark of divinity. In form the figure recalls a statue dating to the Eighteenth Dynasty that represents Tiye, the mother of Akhenaten and principal wife of Amenhotep III. Tiye wears the double uraeus with the head of a vulture in the centre of the headdress, thus stressing both her individuality and her divine status. On the Turin statue there is no distinction between the head of the vulture and those of the flanking cobras, leaving some doubt as to whether two or three cobras were intended. The features of the individual portrayed in this statue are similar to those on the non-Egyptian statues of Cleopatra VII and also to the head of a statue recently retrieved from the harbour at Alexandria and identified as either Caesarion or Octavian.

Some Ptolemaic rulers had good reason to change their cult titles and possibly also their visual representations to reflect their changing consorts. A modern analogy is offered by Camilla, styled Her Royal Highness the Duchess of Cornwall on her marriage to the Prince of Wales in 2005. The title distinguishes Camilla from the Prince's late first wife, Diana, publicly known as Princess of Wales. Like Cleopatra II, who changed her cult affiliation from Philometor (mother-loving) to Euergetes (the one who does good works), and then back to Philometor when the queen enjoyed a much happier life after the exile of her second husband, Cleopatra VII changed her affiliations part-way through her reign. In contrast to the earlier queen Arsinoe II, whose attributes remained constant once established during her lifetime, both Cleopatras II and VII found themselves in positions of change. Another Cleopatra (III) effectively started a new period of rule as consort to her two sons.

Following the birth of Caesarion, Cleopatra VII similarly adopted a new consort; she too most likely developed a new style of presentation to mark the new era of joint rule. Evidence for the early part of her reign may be found on a statue that may be dated on stylistic grounds to the later first century BC (Plate 23). The statue is preserved from the head to the waist. It was found in Fouah, in the Delta, and is now housed in Alexandria. The expression is archaic, the smile forced as on images of the early Ptolemies, but the face retains a certain youthfulness that appears elsewhere in Cleopatra VII's imagery. The queen wears a tripartite wig with a diadem supporting a single uraeus and is dressed in the usual knotted garment; the heavy folds and serrated fringe of the mantle suggest that the piece is late Ptolemaic in date. The back pillar is also similar to that on the statues with a triple uraeus; indeed there are two more examples with this feature. One is now in the Royal Ontario Museum, Toronto, and shows a more stylised version of the Alexandrian portrait; the subject also wears the tripartite wig but with a sheath-like dress. The other is a statue that may well have been deliberately damaged: a colossal granite figure from the festival city Canopus, located to the east of Alexandria and the focus of Roman denunciations of Cleopatra's self-indulgent and immoral lifestyle. The statue stands today in Alexandria's Greco-Roman Museum (Plate 24). The face appears to have been deliberately removed. The hair and body of the piece are preserved enough to show the distinctively high back pillar that appears on the Hermitage, Metropolitan and Brooklyn statues. Like these three, the figure from Canopus combines Egyptian form with Greek features. Here the artist has juxtaposed the Greek corkscrew wig with an Egyptian knotted costume, which itself has folds of drapery reflecting Greek repertoire. The knotted garment and wig suggest that this statue represented a deified Ptolemaic queen. If this was an image of Cleopatra, who removed the face, and was this indeed a deliberate act?

Despite Octavian's victory at Actium and the resulting dramatic change of regime in Egypt, Cleopatra's images did not suffer damnation at the hands of her successor. Quite the contrary seems to have been true both in Rome and Egypt. The statue of the queen that was set up in the Temple of

94

Venus Genetrix in the centre of Rome by Julius Caesar was still visible to historians writing in the second and third centuries AD (though one of these suggests that Octavian looted it from Alexandria). In Egypt at Denderah and Koptos, where Cleopatra decorated a temple and shrine wall with her images, those of her victorious Roman enemy Octavian (later Augustus) were simply placed close by. Indeed in Egypt the queen continued to be worshipped as a goddess until the fourth century AD, and it is unlikely that the priests would have been willing to replace her image with that of her successor. Earlier Egyptian kings had done just this, but it has to be remembered that Augustus was an absent pharaoh and one with very little apparent understanding of or interest in the meaning of the Egyptian cultural tradition. Like all shrewd politicians he seems to have given generously to the temples and priests, thus ensuring that the Egyptian aristocracy would support their new ruler and governor. If, as it appears, the colossus from Canopus was deliberately mutilated, this is likely to have been the work of Christian iconoclasts rather than the first Roman emperor. Roman outrage at the licentious behaviour of Cleopatra and Antony at Canopus was directed at a Roman rather than an Egyptian audience, and there is textual and recently recovered archaeological evidence for widespread Christian destruction of Egyptian sacred images in the shrines of Canopus.

Cleopatra's temples

Like other aspects of the queen's presentation, the temples dedicated during Cleopatra VII's reign served both political and religious functions. The reliefs decorating their walls showed the royal family offering to the gods of Egypt – indeed, sometimes members of their own family were represented among the gods, celebrating the rulers' membership of the Egyptian pantheon. The inner walls show an intimate association of the ruler with the divine; but these were seen only by the priests, who tended to the gods. The outer walls served a different, more public audience. A ruler's piety was thus also a display of his or her power and authority. However, it is always difficult to estimate the extent of the ruler's role against that of the Egyptian priesthood in deciding to dedicate a temple to a particular god. Some regal authority is assumed in deciding where finances should be directed. Indeed Cleopatra's choice of temples – of Hathor at Denderah, of Geb at Koptos, of Montu at Armant and to Julius Caesar in Alexandria – seem to echo her political and personal life on several different levels. It has recently been argued that the queen's dedications at the two Upper Egyptian temples – Denderah and Armant – were quite deliberate and obvious choices reflecting her personal history.

Denderah

The south wall of the Temple of Hathor at Denderah houses one of Cleopatra's best-known images. The temple provided a firm political link with her deceased father: the programme of construction at Denderah was started by Ptolemy Auletes in 54 BC, but the temple remained undecorated at the time of his death. As his rightful heir, the queen 'completed' his project and her image was placed on the outer wall. However, this famous relief of Cleopatra VII and her son Caesarion, both named in accompanying cartouches, displays her allegiance to her co-ruler rather than to the memory of her deceased father. It has been suggested that this focus stresses the link between Cleopatra's personal position and that of the goddess to whom the temple was dedicated. For the myth of Hathor and her son Ihy, with the absent father figure of Horus, was particularly pertinent to Cleopatra and the situation in which she found herself following the birth of her son Caesarion. In any display of potential political impact, Cleopatra's consorts were carefully chosen, and, while it made sense for the queen to link herself to her father in the early part of her reign, in the later years of her reign Caesarion provided her with a vision of Egypt's future. Moreover, 'king's mother' was arguably a stronger role to play than royal princess or even queen. In the event, her dreams were never realised and, as in the shrine of Geb at Koptos, Cleopatra's images would in time share the wall space with those of her enemy Octavian. At the Geb shrine, however, the identity of the Ptolemaic male figure who accompanies the queen is less certain than at Denderah (see below).

Armant

The monuments of Armant were disturbed during both ancient and more recent times. The Temple of Montu and so-called birth-house (*mammisi*) of Cleopatra VII were dismantled during the reign of Antoninus Pius (AD 138-161) to provide blocks for re-use in the monumental arch honouring the Roman emperor. Some of these blocks show the goddess Isis; they can be dated to the late Ptolemaic period on stylistic grounds. Then, during the Late Antique period, a church was built, again re-using blocks from the earlier structures. Visitors to the site today will find no traces of the original birth-house, which suffered the further indignity of being stripped of its blocks which were used to build the nearby sugar-cane factory, now the staple industry in this small town. It has been suggested that the birth-house was built in three phases and that it presented a highly unusual architectural form, constituting Cleopatra's largest project outside Alexandria.

The nineteenth-century scholar Lepsius recorded the title 'female Horus' for Cleopatra VII at Armant. She was not the first Ptolemaic queen to use this title, but its use here reflects the power held by the queen and offers an insight into how she was viewed by Egyptian priests. Unlike the Romans, the upper echelons of Egyptian society were able to adapt to a female ruler; Egypt had a long history of doing so, and Cleopatra as the king's mother and co-ruler enjoyed a powerful position.

Although the temple and birth-house no longer survive, Cleopatra's association with the Egyptian cults at Armant is well documented. A stela dated to 51 BC tells us that the queen took a special interest in the cult of the Buchis bull there, 'rowing him in the barque of Amun together with the royal boats'. As noted above, it has recently been suggested that the queen's interest in the temples at Armant was focused and reflective of her own position. The principal deity worshipped at Armant was Montu, god of war.

The son of Montu was usually called Harpocrates, a version of the young Horus often accompanied by his mother Isis. The usual father of Horus/Harpocrates was Osiris, but a variant of the myth was, it appears, significantly adopted by Cleopatra. Osiris was directly associated with the deceased king of Egypt, the father of the current pharaoh. Cleopatra as Isis had a problem: Julius Caesar was allegedly the father of her child Caesarion/Horus, but he had not ruled Egypt as its king. It is also likely that Cleopatra would have seen her own father as the most obvious candidate for the role of Osiris, but he was not the father of her child, the new king. The difficulty for Cleopatra was that she had effectively taken the role of Horus, traditionally allocated to a male ruler, and her child had been fathered by a foreign ruler. Caesar's personal military distinction and the militarised state of Egypt after Cleopatra's restoration to the throne in 48 BC made Montu the war-god a perfect substitute for the missing father. A recent interpretation of the temple reliefs on these lines offers a fascinating insight into how the Egyptian priesthood could have served as advisors to Cleopatra. Above all else it shows that they were more than willing to help her out of her unconventional personal situation.

The structure at Armant was a substantial one. A recent reconstruction shows three distinct but joined rooms that must have provided a separate centre for cult activity. It has been suggested that the function of the temple was a *mammisi* or birth-house: as such it linked Cleopatra the mother to the mother-goddess Isis. Lepsius recorded a temple relief (now lost to the sugar factory) showing the birth of the divine child in the presence of a male god wearing the crown typically associated with Amun-Re; a female goddess who is often identified as Nekhbet, and Cleopatra, who raises her hands in adoration (Fig. 6). The queen wears the royal uraeus and the double plumed crown, thus appearing as a divine queen rather than a goddess, and thereby avoiding any confusion with Isis in this context.

To summarise, Cleopatra took the title 'father-loving' early in her reign in order to link herself to her father, but following the birth of Caesarion, the queen did her utmost to promote her son and heir, and, rather than ignore the unconventional manner in which he had been created, she played upon this factor to elevate his importance and status. The priests, it seems, were all too happy to find a suitable means to express Caesarion's origins in Egyptian mythology.

Despite the destruction, there are still traces of Cleopatra at Armant. The main temple complex has recently been cleared to reveal several fragments of a monumental gateway or doorway with the cartouche of Cleopatra VII preserved. On the inside walls of one of the temples are reliefs showing a male ruler named simply 'Pharaoh' in the cartouches, a common feature during the early Roman period, found on temples dedicated by Augustus and his immediate successors. There are several images of a late Ptolemaic king (or kings) with different cartouches. One of the names matches that on the shrine of Geb at Koptos. A full reconstruction of the temple is awaited to understand the surviving remains at Armant, but it is already clear that Cleopatra's presence has not been totally erased.

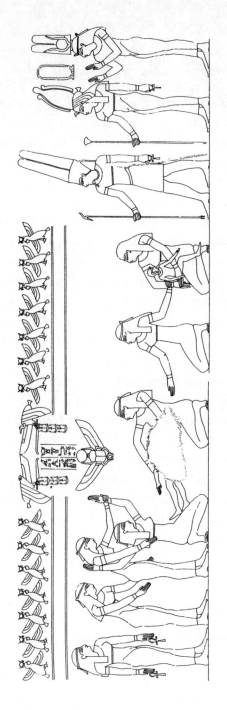

6. *Drawing of the birth-scene in the Mammisi at Armant (after Lepsius).*

The Temple to Julius Caesar in Alexandria

As previously noted, the status of Caesar in Egypt is extremely difficult to understand. His position could have been elevated on account of his role as the presumed father of the pharaoh Ptolemy XV Caesarion. However, modern historians tend to interpret the value of the association in the opposite direction – that is, it was solely in Cleopatra's interests to link her son with the Romans as the child of their Dictator, who two years after his assassination in 44 BC was declared a god in Rome. Nonetheless, the temple dedicated to Julius Caesar in Alexandria celebrated his elevation to a status more suited to the father of her child. Better to be a god than simply a foreign ruler. It was very much in Octavian's interests to support the idea of Caesar's divinity. Like many of Cleopatra's other projects, the temple was completed by him following her death in 30 BC.

Of particular interest is the fragment of a statue in the Egyptian style recently recovered from Alexandria harbour. It may well be associated with the site of the temple to Caesar, although it is not possible to know when the statue was discarded. Identified as either Octavian or Caesarion, it appears from the excavator's reports that the statue had literally been pushed over. The facial features are youthful and similar to some of the statues that have been identified as images of Cleopatra VII. Any confusion with Caesarion – if apparent in antiquity – may have been advantageous to Octavian in an Alexandrian context.

According to ancient literary sources, the two obelisks known today as 'Cleopatra's Needles' once marked the entrance to the temple (Fig. 7). Originally belonging to the Egyptian king Thutmose III, these monuments were moved to Alexandria from the abandoned sanctuary of Atun at Heliopolis by Augustus in AD 13, an interesting development suggesting an established Egyptian presence by that date at the site of Caesar's temple. We know from other sanctuaries such as the early Ptolemaic Temple of Sarapis in the southern part of Alexandria and the sanctuary of Isis (p. 104), that the combination of Egyptian sculpture with Greek architecture was common in the city. The presence of an Egyptian-style statue of Cleopatra's son suggests that perhaps the same was true of the temple to his father. The presence of Egyptian-style statues in a Greek architectural setting conjures up a vision of Egyptian actors performing on a Greek stage-set.

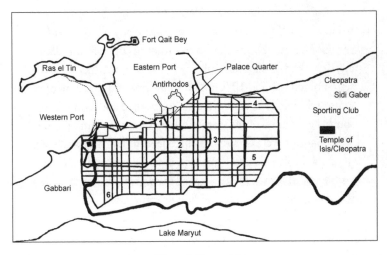

7. Map of Alexandria.

1 Caesareum; 2 Kom el Dikka; 3 Rosetta Gate; 4 Chatby Cemetery; 5 Hadra Cemetery; 6 Sarapieion.

The Temple to Isis in Alexandria

The statue from the Temple of Isis in Alexandria and the identity of the accompanying male figure have already been
discussed in some detail (pp. 91-2), but what of the site and its
nature? At present we must rely on nineteenth-century descriptions because the exact location is not known for certain (Fig.
7). It is hoped that non-invasive survey techniques will rectify
this in the future, but the temple site shares the situation of
most of ancient Alexandria, which lies beneath the modern city.

In 1737 a British visitor named Richard Pococke described
what he saw in an account published by Sir John Gardner
Wilkinson in *Modern Egypt and Thebes*, vol. 1 (1843):

> He [Pococke] mentions ruins of an ancient temple under the
> water about 2 miles from Alexandria which he conjectures
> belonged to Zephyrium or some other place on the road to
> Nicopolis. Pococke saw there a few columns three feet in diam-
> eter [*c.* 90 cm], shattered sphinxes of yellow marble, a female
> statue of red granite, 12 feet high [3.60 cm] with a fragment of
> a colossal male. The remains of a large portico and a little to the
> south a great number of granite columns from a round temple.
> The columns were fluted and three feet in diameter and were
> of course Ptolemaic and Roman in date. Other remains are also
> visible and the rock at the edge of the water was cut in such a
> way as to indicate a great building of some kind.

The statues mentioned by Wilkinson were 'discovered' by
Anthony Harris, British consul in 1840, and removed from the
site. In 1892 some preliminary 'excavations' took place at the
site, recorded by Albert Daninos. The torso of the female and

a pair of hands were taken from the site by Daninos, who attempted, but failed to interest the Musée du Louvre in the statue. In 1912 these two fragments were sold to the Royal Museums of Mariemont in Belgium and remain there today (Plate 22a). The head and left leg of the male statue were installed in the gardens of the Greco-Roman Museum in Alexandria in 1907 and remain there today (Plate 22b). Several fragments of both statues that were recorded in Harris's drawings are missing, though part of a foot has recently been recognised in Alexandria.

The early descriptions of the sanctuary suggest that it had both Greek and Egyptian architectural features. Granite columns and sphinxes found during excavations at the end of the nineteenth century would have echoed the Egyptian nature of the two colossal statues from the site. However, the use of a *tholos* or round temple is part of the Hellenistic Greek tradition and, significantly, one associated with royal cults in Greece. Both the sculptural decoration and the architectural features must have made this one of the city's most impressive monuments. The location to the east of the city centre is testimony to the growing extent of the city, which the Roman traveller and writer Strabo said had spread to the neighbouring site of Canopus by the time of Cleopatra. There is no doubt from the scale of the statues and the size of this site that this was one of the queen's most important and largest projects.

Koptos

The modern visitor to Qift (ancient Koptos) is appropriately greeted by paintings of Cleopatra as she is perceived today at each end of the town's centre. The ancient shrine associated with Cleopatra stands apart from the main temple, cut off by the modern road that runs through the neighbouring village, and is small in comparison to the site as a whole. However, in ritual terms the shrine was extremely important because this was where the sacred barque, the means of transporting gods between temples, would rest.

As at Denderah, it is possible that Cleopatra continued to support her dead father's projects at Koptos. A fragment of the cartouche of Ptolemy XII was found at the main temple site. He built a gateway in the temple enclosure wall leading to the shrine of Geb, which is decorated on the inside with reliefs of Cleopatra, accompanied by an unidentified male ruler. Some scholars believe that this figure represents Auletes himself, while others identify the male as Ptolemy XIII or XIV, either one of her younger brothers and co-rulers in the early years of her reign. The debate was recently reopened but has not been unequivocally solved. The problem lies with the cartouches (royal titles) that appear on the relief representations. One cartouche in the shrine of Geb matches one of those found at Armant, which may well suggest that the two brothers used the same titles as rulers. Many have assumed that the cartouches at Koptos were solely used by Ptolemy XII, and their presence on the walls of the Geb shrine may therefore be seen as evidence of a co-regency between father and daughter. Unfortunately the cartouches of the brothers of Cleopatra – Ptolemies XIII and XIV – are not fully understood: it is believed that they shared titles with each other and their father. Some have concluded that the male consort of Cleopatra at Koptos was her brother Ptolemy XIV, with whom she ruled prior to the birth of Caesarion, if we accept that he was born in 44 BC. An inscription on the crown of a statue from the site only adds to the difficulty of interpreting the remains from Koptos. The crown, now in the Petrie Museum of Egyptian Archaeology, London, was originally part of a limestone statue of a Ptolemaic queen. Her identity is, like that of Cleopatra's consort, much disputed – a common occurrence in the challenging academic field of interpreting Ptolemaic royal statuary.

The Koptos crown

Originally gilded, the Koptos crown consists of double plumes, a sun disk, and cow's horns – the last, like the gilding, now lost. This is the general-purpose crown worn by the majority of Ptolemaic queens; it is also the crown that Cleopatra wears on the Denderah reliefs and on the decorated walls of the Geb shrine.

The crown was originally thought to be from a statue of Arsinoe II on account of the titles on the back pillar, which read:

Hereditary noble,	King's daughter,
great praise,	King's sister,
mistress of Upper and Lower Egypt,	great royal wife,
contented.	who satisfies the heart of Horus.

The lower section of the inscription, including the queen's name, is unfortunately missing. Although Arsinoe II fulfilled the criteria for the titles in column 2 in that she was married to her brother, the crown is not of a type known to have been worn by Arsinoe II. Moreover, Arsinoe I, Ptolemy II's first wife, was exiled to Koptos following the return of his sister to Egypt. It is conceivable that the ruler and priests dedicated a statue to her successor at the temple, but it seems an insensitive act. If, then, the crown was not from a statue of Arsinoe II, which queen did it mark? Not all rulers married their sisters. Out of all of the royal women there were only Arsinoe II, Arsinoe III, wife of Ptolemy IV; Cleopatra II, wife of Ptolemies VI and VIII; Cleopatra Berenike III, who was referred to as the sister of her in fact uncle Ptolemy X; Cleopatra Tryphaena, wife of Ptolemy XII; Cleopatra VII, who was married to Ptolemies XIII and XIV. The crown has another identifiable feature – three uraei rather the usual single royal cobra. Once again the association of the crown with Arsinoe II cannot be upheld, because Arsinoe wore the double uraeus (see p. 84). It has, however, been suggested that Cleopatra VII may have worn the triple cobra.

The crown may help to solve the problem of identifying Cleopatra's consort at Koptos, if indeed it can be associated with this particular queen. Ultimately, however, the identity of the wearer resides in the named lower crown, now lost.

Cleopatra's tomb

The early Ptolemaic rulers were buried with Alexander the Great in Alexandria. By the time of Ptolemy IV the royal tomb and associated sanctuaries had been rebuilt and refashioned with a pyramidal roof. Cleopatra, however, seems to have chosen a new site for her tomb. The literary sources describe the mausoleum of Cleopatra as a two-storey building to which the queen fled, seeking refuge from Octavian and the invading Roman forces. The structure was still under construction at the time of Alexandria's fall to Rome in 30 BC; by means of the ropes used by the builders Cleopatra was able to lift the dying Mark Antony up to the second level. We also know from ancient writers that there was a sanctuary of Isis attached to the tomb, evidence of Cleopatra's intention to continue the Ptolemaic tradition of the royal cults.

The fact that the queen selected a new site for her mausoleum might even suggest that she intended it to function as a traditional Egyptian mortuary temple. Perhaps during one of her trips to Upper Egypt she saw such temples that had been dedicated by earlier Egyptian rulers including Hatshepsut, the female king of the Eighteenth Dynasty, and, as previously mentioned (p. 82), the temple-tomb of the Twenty-fifth Dynasty god's wife Shepenwepet at Medinat Habu.

Recently attempts have been made to reconstruct Cleopatra's mausoleum digitally, from the evidence for its use offered by ancient writers. The result is a Hellenistic Greek-style two-storey podium tomb; unfortunately this cannot be corroborated by the literary sources, in which the actual appearance of the building is not described. One would imagine that the known link with Isis might well have demanded an Egyptian-style monument or at least one that in some way acknowledged the Egyptian tradition. In 2003 it was tentatively suggested that the colossal dyad showing Cleopatra with a male consort (Plate 22) may well have been associated with the queen's mausoleum. As noted above (p. 104), descriptions of the site of its discovery by nineteenth-century travellers mention a large 'edifice' and also a rock-cut chamber that was full of water as a result of the rising water table.

Cleopatra's consorts in Egypt

In Egypt Cleopatra was associated as ruler with various family members. First her father, with whom it has been suggested she ruled jointly during the final years of his reign; then her two younger brothers, Ptolemy XIII and Ptolemy XIV. The first of these proved to be an ill-suited match, and we have no evidence to suggest that the two promoted themselves actively during the early part of the queen's reign: on the contrary, Ptolemy XIII's courtiers drove Cleopatra into exile. The younger brother ruled with Cleopatra as her equal, in theory at least, but it is very clear that it was the queen who decided the movements of her brother. Had Ptolemy XIV been older and wiser, or had there been a politically powerful member of the royal court to act as regent, the young king might well have stayed in Egypt during his sister's two-year sojourn in Rome and seized the opportunity to gain control of the country, then occupied by three, and ultimately four of Caesar's legions. Instead Ptolemy XIV died shortly after his return to Egypt, clearing the path for the son of Cleopatra and Julius Caesar to rule with his mother. It is interesting that, although mother and son are each awarded a certain degree of autonomy on temple reliefs, the other is never far away (Plate 19).

A similar link can quite possibly be seen in statuary in the round. There are several surviving portraits widely recognised as young late Ptolemaic princes, which are in fact likely to represent the young Caesarion. Stylistically they are very similar to the statues discussed earlier in this chapter which show a queen with a triple uraeus. The characteristic down-turned mouth, strong chin and wide brow feature on nearly all of the examples. On some of these images the softer model-ling of the mouth echoes one of the categories of images bearing a triple uraeus. Many show the ruler with a diadem and uraeus rather than the traditional nemes head-cloth. On one example, retrieved from the harbour of Alexandria, close to the Temple of Caesar, there are sockets suited to the attach-ment of horns, stressing the young ruler's ties with the god Amun (Greek Ammon). In this way a mutual promotion and also association of Cleopatra and Caesarion was presented to the people of Egypt.

In the international sphere, however, it is clear that Cleopatra really held the power. The queen appears on coinage either by herself or alongside Mark Antony; the only time that Caesarion appears is on coinage minted in Cyprus (Plate 10a), thought to celebrate his birth. His image is preserved as a small blob, representing his head as his divine mother nurses him.

Cleopatra as an Egyptian queen in Rome

In Egypt Cleopatra was shown as an Egyptian ruler. However, her international image offers proof that she was able to adapt her royal presentation to suit the local audience. One of the finest examples of Cleopatra's adaptability was found rebuilt in a later church wall built on the site of an early sanctuary of Isis on the Esquiline hill in Rome. The image may well have been dedicated by Cleopatra herself or in her honour during her two-year stay in Rome. Now brilliantly displayed in a former power station on the Via Ostiense, the Centro Montemartini of the Capitoline Museums, the figure is preserved as a marble bust, which would originally have been slotted into a body perhaps made from coloured stone. It is interesting from many points of view.

This image is one of the earliest examples of a phenomenon that became extremely popular following the Roman occupation of Egypt: the production in Rome and elsewhere of art in the Egyptian style. Such objects are essentially classical in terms of material and form – statues for example are mostly made of white marble, do not have a dorsal support, nor do they stride forward in the usual Egyptian fashion. The medium was however influenced by the Egyptian tradition. The Esquiline bust provides an image that can be recognised as Egyptian, but was clearly manufactured as a portrait of its subject and with a lively Hellenistic Greek interpretation of the usually stylised wig and headdress. The subject wears a vulture headdress; the wings and tail are carved in a naturalistic way – more so than their Egyptian counterparts – with carefully rendered feathering. There are two holes cut in the upper surface: the first where the neck and head of the vulture would once have been slotted into place, and the second on top of the head, where a crown would have been placed. The latter hole is too shallow to support the size and proportion of crown expected for an Egyptian statue, and so it is likely that this feature too was rendered at a scale more comfortably associated with the figure's Roman context.

The facial features have much in common with the other

portraits of Cleopatra surviving from Rome. They are youthful, idealised and regal in appearance, qualities accentuated here by the contrast between these features and the formulaic Egyptian wig. In many early catalogues this bust was described as a representation of the goddess Isis, and that is precisely its identity. However, the bust has more recently been acknowledged as a portrait of a Ptolemaic queen. The hitherto unrecognised personal features of Cleopatra VII add to its importance, for they suggest a direct link between the queen and the cult of Isis in Rome. The replication of the figure at miniature scale on finger rings intended for wear by individual devotees suggests that the statue and its subject were an important part of this religious development.

Egyptian statues in Rome

There was, however, another way in which the legacy of the deified Cleopatra and her ancestors survived in Rome. Their images not only lived on but were even worshipped, in a manner that could not have been contrived more successfully had Cleopatra planned it herself. During the first century AD Egyptian cults became extremely popular in Italy, and certain emperors promoted gods such as Isis and Sarapis with a renewed vigour that was ironically not matched by their patronage of temples in Egypt. Statues were imported from Egypt to Rome in order to decorate sanctuaries and Roman versions of Egyptian images were produced in Italy. This latter category of images was Egyptianising rather than strictly adhering to Egyptian models, adapting rather than adopting already established forms. Nowhere is this more apparent than in the development of the image of the goddess Isis, who had, it must be remembered, a rather conventional Egyptian form that could have been accepted with ease into the Roman repertoire.

During the Hellenistic Greek period, cults of Isis outside Egypt were centred on a statue that was similar in presentation to that of any other Greek goddess. The Hellenised deity wore a simple tunic (*chiton*) and mantle (*himation*) and was probably and quite correctly associated with the goddess of love, Aphrodite. Her treatment by the Romans marks the essential difference between the two cultures. Rome was keen to promote the Egyptian origins of Isis, not in their pure form, but rather to adapt the goddess's presentation so that a Roman viewer could read the images and to some extent claim the goddess as one of his or her own pantheon. At the same time a sense of Isis' eastern origins was also required as a main feature of her cult. We see this in Egyptian sanctuaries outside Rome, where, as in the metropolis, statues were imported from Egypt to serve the new cults. Thus any visitors to the temple would immediately be swept eastwards, and reminded of the origins of the gods that they were worshipping.

The major changes in the presentation of Isis seem to have occurred during the reign of Domitian (AD 81-96). The emperor himself never visited Egypt, nor, interestingly, did he patronise any large-scale building projects in the province in comparison to the efforts of other Roman emperors. However, aged eighteen in AD 69, the Year of the Four Emperors, Domitian had escaped the conflicts raging around the Capitol of Rome dressed as a priest of Isis. On lamps dating to the end of the first century AD, Isis appears wearing a knotted garment, a sun disk and a crown of cow's horns with the double plume. Her hair is typically styled with loose locks falling onto her shoulders. A hundred years earlier, this image had represented deified Ptolemaic queens. It had been adopted by priestesses in Egypt, and was now supporting the presentation of Isis in the Roman world. Cleopatra's image had survived another hundred years.

Cleopatra in Late Antique and early Arab/Muslim Egypt

Only in Egypt itself and in areas of Ptolemaic influence, if not outright control, has Cleopatra enjoyed a consistently good press. Here she is seen even today as a wise and patriotic ruler, whose machinations with her Roman lovers and patrons were no more than the expression of her love for the country for which she found herself responsible.

In the third century AD, Cleopatra's patriotism was pressed into service by Queen Zenobia of Palmyra in Syria, who led a revolt against Rome in AD 270 and styled herself 'the new Cleopatra'. A century later, when the Roman Empire had long since officially adopted Christianity, a graffito inscribed on the Temple of Isis at Philae in Upper Egypt recorded the worship of Cleopatra. In this Nubian stronghold traditional Egyptian culture survived longer than elsewhere, and it is here that Cleopatra may have been formally worshipped for the last time. Nonetheless, the sixth-century Coptic bishop John of Nikiou, a native Egyptian, praised the queen's wisdom and strength of character, as 'the most illustrious and wise among women', and four centuries later the Arab historian Al-Masudi characterised Cleopatra as 'the last of the wise ones of Greece'. Indeed Arab Egyptian tradition paid as much extravagant attention to Cleopatra's alleged intellectual achievements as the West has paid to her alleged voluptuous sexuality and voracious appetite for pleasure and profit. Thus Cleopatra was credited with the construction of the famous Pharos or lighthouse at Alexandria, one of the seven wonders of the ancient world, and a defensive wall protecting all Egypt from invaders; learned works on philosophy, meteorology, medicine, alchemy and cosmetics were also ascribed to the queen. With the possible exception of blocks from the Pharos, a monument commissioned by Cleopatra's distant predecessors, none of these works survives. However, the eastern emphasis on Cleopatra's learning surely reflects her high intelligence and sound education, both qualities noted in the surviving ancient sources, and stands in significant contrast to the erotic celebrity evoked by Hollywood.

Beyond Cleopatra herself, the wider picture of the fate of the Ptolemies is less positive. During the Late Antique period temple reliefs decorated with images of the Ptolemaic royal house were systematically destroyed or damaged, among them dedications made by Cleopatra VII. The Ptolemaic royal cults were able to survive the initial Roman invasion, but the longer established Egyptian cults could not withstand dwindling imperial interest from the third century AD. As the old religion made way for Christianity and fewer Roman emperors were interested in promoting their image in the province, many of the Egyptian temples lost essential support from their ever more distant rulers. The structures were stripped for building material or changed their function.

Thus, for example, a pottery workshop was set up in the temple of the king-maker Ptah at Memphis in the late Roman period, and in some cases Coptic monasteries were founded where pagan priests once lived.

The inscriptional evidence paints a similarly bleak picture of Egyptian culture in that the use of demotic (a cursive hieroglyphic form) and also dedications made in Greek were in a state of gradual decline. Material culture, however, did not adapt quite as fast as language, and traces remain of the Egyptian culture that had flourished under the Ptolemies and the Roman emperors of the first two centuries AD. Unlike with the images of Isis made in the early Roman period, it is not possible to make direct links between Cleopatra's image and those adopted subsequently to represent new subjects of worship.

However, some suggestive comparisons are hard to resist. The most obvious successor to Cleopatra and her elder son as Isis and Horus is the image of the Virgin Mary nursing the infant Jesus. While it is possible that the iconographic link between the two pairs can be substantiated, it is most likely that any resemblance concerns Isis rather than the queen herself.

We find a similar case when we consider the use of images of certain Greek deities who remained popular into the fourth century and beyond. Dionysos and his entourage remained a common decorative element on bone panels that formed a part of caskets or boxes. The god of wine was closely linked with the Ptolemaic royal house and their presentation to their subjects: we may recall Cleopatra's father's use of the epithet 'the new Dionysos' and Mark Antony's appearance as Dionysos in Alexandria in 34 BC. The goddess Hygeia, the personification of health, can be found on similar panels with a snake (a link to Asklepios), wearing a *stephane* or crown and with her hair often styled in a fashion reminiscent of Cleopatra's image in the Greek and Roman worlds.

It is unlikely that we can prove, or indeed realistically suggest, a direct link between these iconographic features and Cleopatra VII. However, it is possible that artists drew upon earlier traditions and material and that somewhere there was a visual counterpart to the evidently strong literary memory of the last Ptolemaic ruler. Unlike the adoption of the images of Ptolemaic queens for those of the goddess Isis in early imperial Rome, there is no evidence to suggest that original representations of Cleopatra were utilised in the fourth century AD and later. Even following the Arab invasion in AD 642, Cleopatra's memory survived in a written rather than representational mode; hence the need to reinvent images of the queen in the medieval manuscripts of Europe.

Following the Arab invasion of Egypt in AD 642, the capital was moved to a new site, Fustat, part of modern Cairo. The move seems to have been dictated by a shift in trade from the Mediterranean to the Red Sea region rather than an overtly political motivation. The result, however, was that Alexandria suffered: the city that Alexander the Great had founded and which was subsequently developed by Cleopatra, her ancestors and their successors, was no longer the seat of power. In many ways the new capital city mirrored its predecessor, and in many respects the incoming rulers used Alexandria as a model for their new city. The continuing influence of Alexandria can be clearly seen on the minaret of the ninth-century AD mosque of the governor of Egypt and

Syria, Ahmad Ibn Tulun, which takes the form of the Pharos, one of the wonders of ancient Alexandria. In seventh-century writings Cleopatra was herself named as the builder of the lighthouse and its inclusion in the design of the mosque might even be seen as a direct reference to her.

It is of little surprise that the new Arab regime should seek to include historical figures from ancient Egypt, for unstated motives – whether asserting the country's distinguished past as the home of scientific advances, or attempting to link their own considerable interest in science and engineering to the history of the newly conquered state. In this process of cultural assimilation, Cleopatra played a key intellectual role. In her own country, Cleopatra's journey was altogether different from the western construct of the extravagant and wilful ruler, whose moral turpitude was only partly redeemed by her suicide for love of Antony.

5

Coda: The Meaning of Cleopatra's Death

It has been suggested that Cleopatra's VII's chosen method of suicide – death from the bite of a cobra – was deliberate. Furthermore, the number of snakes – at least two in order to kill the queen herself and then her two servants – might have been celebrating an association clearly noted on Ptolemaic statues. This idea is an interesting one, but at the same time is fraught with ideological difficulties.

The royal cobra represented the eye of the sun-god Ra, and as such was intended to protect the wearer. During the Ptolemaic period the right to wear the uraeus was limited to either royal or divine figures; however, following the Roman occupation of Egypt, like many ideological symbols that were previously reserved for the higher echelons of society, the uraeus is found on the funerary wrappings of private individuals. The literary sources refer to a statue of the queen that was carried in Octavian's victory procession, which included a representation of a snake. It is also clear that ancient writers were aware of an alternative to the death by snake-bite theory, and knew that administering poison offered a more practical alternative. Indeed, the notion that the very symbol intended to protect had turned attacker might have been a cruel and ironic twist of fate. It is possible, or indeed likely, that the source of the snake-bite rumour was the Roman camp, which had caused the queen to take her life.

Whether the queen believed she would be reborn in the afterlife is an interesting question. We know that Cleopatra had an understanding of and indeed interest in Egyptian religion, and that in Egypt she was keen to be presented as part of the local pantheon of gods. As with any historical figure, it is impossible to understand her personal beliefs: as historians we are simply left with records and images to evaluate. At least in her death the queen was permitted to be buried with the father of her children, but it is impossible that Mark Antony could have provided an Osiris to her Isis.

Selected Further Reading

This list represents a small fraction of the vast bibliography on Cleopatra. However, the books listed here offer a way into the subject and more detailed bibliography.

General

Sally-Ann Ashton, *The Last Queens of Egypt* (Pearson Longman, London 2003).

R.S. Bianchi (ed.), *Cleopatra's Egypt: Age of the Ptolemies* (Brooklyn Museum of Art, 1988).

Alan Bowman, *Egypt after the Pharaohs* (British Museum Press, London , reprinted 1996).

Michel Chauveau, *Cleopatra Beyond the Myth* (trans. David Lorton, Cornell 2002).

Michael Grant, *Cleopatra: A Biography* (Weidenfeld & Nicolson, London 1972, reprinted 1995).

Lucy Hughes-Hallett, *Cleopatra: Histories, Dreams, Distortions* (Pimlico Press 1990, reprinted 1997).

E.E. Rice, *Cleopatra* (Alan Sutton, Gloucester 1999).

Susan Walker and Sally-Ann Ashton (eds), *Cleopatra Reassessed* (British Museum Press, London 2003).

Susan Walker and Peter Higgs (eds), *Cleopatra of Egypt: From History to Myth* (British Museum Press, London 2001).

Maria Wyke, *The Roman Mistress* (Oxford 2002), esp. pp. 195-320.

Paul Zanker, *The Power of Images in the Age of Augustus* (trans. Alan Schapiro, Ann Arbor, Michigan 1990).

Selected Further Reading

Specific references for points of detail discussed in individual chapters

1. From Heroic Suicide to Banknote Icon: Modern Views of Cleopatra

Ella Shohat, 'Disorienting Cleopatra: a modern trope of identity', in Walker and Ashton (2003), 127-38.

Marie-Stéphanie Delamaire, 'William Wetmore Story's Nubian Cleopatra: Egypt and slavery in nineteenth-century America', in Walker and Ashton (2003), 113-18.

R.S. Bianchi, 'Images of Cleopatra VII reconsidered', in Walker and Ashton (2003), 13-24.

Mary Hamer, 'The myth of Cleopatra since the Renaissance', in Walker and Higgs (2001), 302-11.

2. The Historical Cleopatra

Andrew Meadows, 'Sins of the Fathers: the inheritance of Cleopatra, last queen of Egypt', in Walker and Higgs (2001), 14-31.

Peter van Minnen, 'A royal ordnance of Cleopatra and related documents', in Walker and Ashton (2003), 35-44.

Susan Walker, 'Carry-on at Canopus: the Nilotic mosaic of Palestrina and Roman attitudes to Egypt', in Roger Matthews and Cornelia Roemer (eds), *Ancient Perspectives on Egypt* (UCL Press, London 2003), 191-202;

Susan Walker, *The Portland Vase* (British Museum Press, London 2004).

Herwig Maehler, 'Roman poets on Egypt', in Matthews and Roemer (2003), 203-15.

Marc Étienne, 'Queen, harlot or lecherous goddess? An Egyptological approach to a Roman image of propaganda', in Walker and Ashton (2003), 95-102.

3. Cleopatra's Royal Image in the Greek and Roman World

Susan Walker, 'From Queen of Egypt to Queen of Kings: the portraits of Cleopatra VII', in N. Bonacasa and A.M. Donadoni Roveri (eds), *Faraoni come dei, dei come faraoni. Atti del V Congresso Internazionale Italo-Egiziano, Torino, Archivio di Stato, 8-12 dicembre 2001* (Palermo 2003).

Peter Higgs, 'Searching for Cleopatra's image: classical portraits in stone', in Walker and Higgs (2001), 200-9.

Peter Higgs, 'Resembling Cleopatra: Cleopatra's portraits in the context of late Hellenistic female portraiture', in Walker and Ashton (2003), 57-70.

Peter Higgs and Susan Walker, 'Cleopatra VII at the Louvre', in Walker and Ashton (2003), 71-4.

Jonathan Williams, 'Imperial style in the coins of Cleopatra and Mark Antony', in Walker and Ashton (2003), 87-94.

4. Cleopatra as Queen of Egypt

Sally-Ann Ashton, 'Identifying the Egyptian-style Ptolemaic queens', in Walker and Higgs (2001), 148-152.

Sally-Ann Ashton, 'Cleopatra: goddess, ruler or regent?', in Walker and Ashton (2003), 25-30.

John Ray, 'Cleopatra in the temples of Upper Egypt: the evidence of Dendera and Armant', in Walker and Ashton (2003), 9-12.

Guy Weill Goudchaux, 'Cleopatra's subtle religious strategy', in Walker and Higgs (2001), 128-41.

Günter Grimm, 'Alexandria in the time of Cleopatra' in Walker and Ashton (2003), 45-50.

Okasha El-Daly, ' "The Virtuous Scholar": Queen Cleopatra in medieval Muslim/Arab writings', in Walker and Ashton (2003), 51-4.

Okasha El-Daly, *Egyptology: The Missing Millennium. Ancient Egypt in Arabic Medieval Writing* (UCL Press, London 2005).

Index